1 PE
JAMES

LIVING THROUGH DIFFICULT TIMES

PROJECT ENGINEER:
Lyman Coleman

AUTHOR OF THE COMMENTARY/NOTES
Richard Peace

AUTHORS OF THE GROUP QUESTIONS
Dietrich Gruen
William Cutler
Vern Becker
Mary Naegeli
James Singleton
Denny Rydberg

PRODUCTION TEAM
John Winson
Billie Herwig
Erika Tiepel
Paul Weiland
Doug LaBudde

COVER DESIGN
Steve Eames

CARTOONIST
Robert Shull

SERENDIPITY GROUP BIBLE STUDY

Serendipity GROUP Bible Study Series
SERENDIPITY/BOX 1012/LITTLETON, CO 80160 / **TOLL FREE 800-525-9563**
In Colorado (303) 798-1313

94 95 96 / CHG / 10 9 8 7 6 5 4 3

Questions And Answers About

Starting a Bible Study Group

PURPOSE
1. *What is the purpose of a Bible study group?* Three things: (and all three are important)

   a. Nurture—to be fed by God and grow in Christ, principally through Bible study.

   b. Support—getting to know each other in a deeper way and caring for each other's needs

   c. Mission—reaching out to non-churched people who are open to studying the Bible and reaching beyond your initial number until you can split into two groups . . . and keep multiplying.

NON-CHURCHED
2. *How can people who don't go to church be interested in studying the Bible?* Pretty easy. In a recent survey, the Gallup Poll discovered that 74% of the people in America are looking for a spiritual faith.

TURNED-OFF
3. *Then, why don't they go to church?* Because they have a problem with the institutional church.

SEEKERS
4. *What are you suggesting?* That you start a Bible study group for these kinds of people:

   ● People who are turned off by the church but are looking for a spiritual faith.

   ● People who are struggling with personal problems and need a support group.

   ● People who are crippled by a bad experience with the church and want to start over in their spiritual pilgrimage.

   ● People who are down on themselves and need encouragement to see beyond their own shortcomings.

   ● People who are looking for hope in the face of seemingly insurmountable difficulties.

   ● People who flashed across your mind as you read over this list.

RECRUITING	5. *How do I get started?* Make a list of the "honest seekers you know" and keep this list on your refrigerator until you have asked everyone.
FIRST MEETING	6. *What do we do at the first meeting?* Decide on your group covenant— a "contract" that spells out your expectations and rules (see the center section, page 3).
DEVELOPING A CONTRACT	7. *How do we develop a contract?* Discuss these questions and ask someone to write down what you agree upon. (This "contract" will be used again at the close to evaluate your group).

- What is the purpose of our group?

- What are the specific goals?

- How long are we going to meet? (We recommend 6 to 12 weeks. Then, if you wish to continue, you can renew the contract.)

- Where are we going to meet?

- What is going to be the starting and ending time at the sessions?

- What about babysitting/refreshments/etc.?

LIFECYCLE	8. *How long should a Bible study group last?* This should be taken in stages. (See flow chart below)
SHORT	9. *Why only a few weeks to start with?* Because people will give priority to something if they know it's not for long. And they can always renew and keep going if they wish.
STUDY PLANS	10. *How do we go about the study of this book of the Bible?* This should be decided at the first meeting. Inside the front cover of this book are a number of options that you can choose from. You need to discuss these options and agree on your study plans.

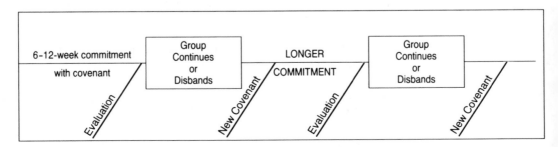

HOMEWORK   11. *Is there any homework?* No—unless you want to do some research about a particular concern. If you are studying one of the longer books of the Bible, where you do not have time to cover every passage, you may want to follow the "Reading" suggestions for this course of study.

BIBLE IGNORANCE   12. *What if we have people in the group who know nothing about the Bible?* Great. This is what this group is all about. There are NOTES on the opposite page to refer to if you have any questions about a word, historical fact or significant person in the passage.

NOTES   13. *Who wrote these Notes?* Richard Peace, a Professor at Gordon Conwell Seminary and a recognized Bible scholar.

SERENDIPITY   14. *What is Serendipity?* A small research foundation that specializes in programs for support groups in a Christian context.

DREAM   15. *What is your dream?* Christian support groups for hurting and struggling people inside and outside of the church—built around a study of Scripture and care for one another. For further information, we invite you to call:
TOLL FREE 800-525-9563, In COLORADO 303-798-1313.

Introduction to

1 PETER

The General Epistles

1 and 2 Peter are what have been called "General" or "Catholic" Epistles. In addition to 1 and 2 Peter, five other books are included in this category: Jude, James, and 1, 2 and 3 John. They were given this designation because it was felt that these letters were *universal* in scope. They were written to *all* churches and not just to a particular church (or person), as were Paul's letters.

However, this is not a completely accurate designation. Both James and 1 Peter are written to specific (though widely scattered) groups of Christians, and 2 and 3 John are addressed to very particular audiences (a specific church in one case and a specific person in the other).

Audience

1 Peter is a circular letter written to Christians living in the northwest section of Asia Minor (in what is now modern Turkey). In 1:1, Peter mentions Pontus, Galatia, Cappadocia, Asia and Bithynia (all of which are Roman provinces). This is a huge area with a large population. The fact that there were Christians living throughout the region testifies to the success of the early Christian missionaries.

The Christians to whom Peter writes were mainly Gentiles, as is clear from the way in which he describes their pre-conversion lifestyle. Peter uses categories and phrases that typically were applied to pagans, not Jews (see 1:14; 2:9-10; 4:3-4). Peter also uses the Greek form of his name in this letter, and not "Simeon," his Jewish name (as in Ac 15:14).

Occasion

Peter wrote this letter to bring hope and strength to men and women who were being persecuted because they were Christians. At the time he wrote, such harassment was new. For the first three decades of its existence, the church was protected, not persecuted, by the Roman Empire. Christianity was seen as a Jewish sect and Judaism was recognized as a legitimate religion.

All this changed on July 19, A. D. 64. That night, Rome caught fire. For three days and three nights the fire blazed out of control. Ancient temples and historic landmarks were swept away by the ferocity of the blaze. Homes were destroyed. Ten of the fourteen wards in the city suffered damage; three were reduced to rubble. The citizens of Rome were distraught and they were angry. They were angry because it was widely felt that Nero, the emperor, was the one responsible for the fire. If he had not actually started it (and there was evidence he did), he certainly had done nothing to contain it. In fact, Suetonius, the Roman historian, wrote that Nero "set fire to the city so openly that several former consuls did not venture to lay hands on his chamberlains although they caught them on their estates with tow and firebands."

Why would Nero burn down the city? Many felt that his passion for building led him to destroy Rome so that he could rebuild it. Nero tried to squelch the rumors about his part in the fire. He provided generous aid to the homeless and he did rebuild the city, this time with parks, wide streets, and buildings constructed of fireproof material. Still the rumors persisted. In desperation, Nero created a scapegoat. He blamed the fire on the Christians. In so doing, Nero introduced the church to martyrdom. The persecution that began in Rome would soon spread across the Empire.

Why were Christians chosen to be the scapegoats? One reason probably had to do with antisemitism. The Jews were not popular in first-century Rome, and Christianity was considered to be a Jewish sect. Another reason had to do with rumors that were circulating about Christian rites. Some said that Christians were cannibals (who each week ate somebody's body and drank someone's blood). Others accused them of orgies, misunderstanding what the Agape (or Love) Feast was all about.

In any case, the persecution directed at Christians was savage. Tacitus, another Roman historian, wrote about the events in that day:

> Neither human resources, nor imperial munificence, nor appeasement of the gods, eliminated sinister suspicions that the fire had been instigated. To suppress this rumor, Nero fabricated scapegoats—and punished with every refinement the notoriously depraved Christians (as they were popularly called)....First, Nero had self-acknowledged Christians arrested. Then, on their information, large numbers of others were condemned—not so much for incendiarism as for their anti-social tendencies. Their deaths were made farcical. Dressed in wild animals' skins, they were torn to pieces by dogs, or crucified, or made into torches to be ignited after dark as substitutes for daylight. Nero provided his Gardens for the spectacle....Despite their guilt as Christians, and the ruthless punishment it deserved, the victims were pitied. For it was felt that they were being sacrificed to one man's brutality rather than to the national interest.

Under Roman law, there were two type of religious systems: those that were legal (such as Judaism) and those that were forbidden. Anyone who practiced a forbidden religion was considered a criminal and was subject to harsh penalties. After the Great Fire, Christianity was declared to be a forbidden religion. This meant that throughout the Empire, Christians were now technically outlaws and thus subject to persecution. Peter writes to those Christians in Asia Minor who were going through such persecution (4:12).

Purpose

Peter wrote this letter to comfort and encourage these Asian Christians in the midst of the "painful trial" (4:12) they were undergoing. He says to them: "Rejoice that you participate in the sufferings of Christ" (4:13). At first glance, this seems to be a strange thing to say. How can they rejoice when times are so tough? The answer Peter gives is that rejoicing is possible because of the great *hope* they have as Christians. Hope is the theme of Peter's letter to these suffering Christians.

Style

1 Peter is written in excellent Greek. So much so that some have questioned whether a Galilean fisherman like Peter could have have such a sophisticated command of the language. 1 Peter contains some of the best Greek in the New Testament—"smoother and more literary than that of the highly trained Paul" (Beare); with a rhythmic structure not unlike that found in the writings of the Greek masters.

As it turns out, this good Greek probably come from a man by the name of Silas. As Peter says in 5:12: "With the help of Silas... I have written to you briefly...." The way the Greek is phrased in 5:12 indicates that Silas was more than a mere stenographer. He could well be the one who helped Peter to polish up the language and style as he dictated the letter. "The thought is the thought of Peter; but the style is the style of Silvanus" (Barclay).

Sources

When reading 1 Peter, one keeps hearing echoes from other parts of the Bible. Certainly the Old Testament is one source which Peter drew upon. He quotes a number of passages, particularly from Isaiah (e.g., 1:24; 2:6,8,22 where he quotes Isa 40:6-8; 28:16; 8:14; 53:9). Furthermore, he makes a lot of allusions to Old Testament ideas and stories (e.g., in 1:19 and 2:4-10, which parallel Isa 53).

Peter also seems to be familiar with the writing of St. Paul. There are parallels to Romans and, in particular, to Ephesians (e.g. compare 1Pe 1:3 with Eph 1:3 and compare 1Pe 1:20 with Eph 1:4; furthermore, the instructions to slaves, husbands, and wives are similar to what is found in Eph 5-6). In addition, there are parallels to Hebrews and James. Not surprisingly, the clearest parallels are to Peter's sermons in Acts. Selwyn has shown that the theology of 1 Peter parallels exactly the theology in these sermons.

Of course, this does not necessarily mean that Peter was consciously quoting from New Testament documents. What he is echoing may simply be the common pattern of teaching in the early church into which he is tapping, as did other New Testament writers.

Date

As with most other ancient letters, it is not possible to give a precise date for the composition of 1 Peter. However, if this letter was sparked by Nero's persecution (and if Peter died in Rome in A.D. 68 as tradition has it), then it must have been written in the mid-60's.

Outline

I. Greetings (1:1-2)
II. The Identity of the People of God (1:3-2:10)
    A. A Great Salvation (1:3-12)
    B. A New Lifestyle (1:13-25)
    C. A Chosen Priesthood (2:1-10)
III. The Responsibilities of the People of God (2:11-4:11)
    A. The Mission of God's People (2:11-12)
    B. Respect: The Key to a Missionary Lifestyle (2:13-3:12)
    C. The Promise of Vindication (3:13-4:6)
    D. Love: The Key to an Eschatological Lifestyle (4:7-11)
IV. The Present Challenge to the People of God (4:12-5:14)
    A. The Fiery Trial (4:12-19)
    B. The Responsibilities of a Church under Judgment (5:1-11)
    C. Conclusion (5:12-14)

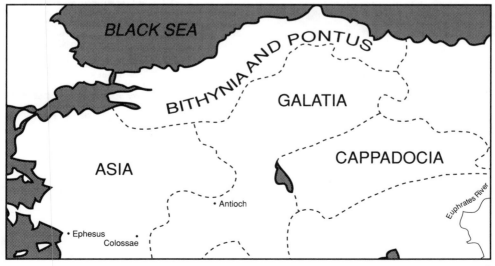

UNIT 1   Salutation

1 Peter 1:1-2

1 Peter, an apostle of Jesus Christ,

To God's elect, strangers in the world, scattered throughout Pontus, Galatia, Cappadocia, Asia and Bithynia, ²who have been chosen according to the foreknowledge of God the Father, through the sanctifying work of the Spirit, for obedience to Jesus Christ and sprinkling by his blood:

Grace and peace be yours in abundance.

Questions

OPEN: 1. As a child, what was one of your favorite "They-lived-happily-ever-after" stories? Why? As an adult, do you read sober and realistic books, or are you still a romantic idealist at heart? **2.** When you cross the midpoint on a trip (or training session), are you more likely to say, "We're halfway there," or "We still have just as far to go"? Why? **3.** Right now, would you describe your progress in the Christian life by talking about how far you've come, or about how far you have to go? How far along the way are you, anyway?

DIG: Read the Introduction and leaf through 1 Peter. Note captions and other clues about the book's meaning. **1.** What are some of the things to look for in this book? What are your first impressions? What are the key ideas? The common refrains? **2.** Examine the following: 4:1-4, 12-16 and 5:8-9. What problems were these believers facing? What questions must have been in their minds? **3.** If 1 Peter were dropped from the Bible, what would be missing from the story of God's redemptive work in history?

REFLECT: 1. Imagine that as of today, Christianity is outlawed. All churches and related ministries are forbidden. What pressures would you face? What would you do about your pastor? About the missionaries you support? About the activities of the church? What would you say if (and when) you were questioned about your faith? **2.** Of the various reasons for hope and commands to act, which one means the most to you when you face difficulties? Why? In what way can the group pray for you as you hold on to that hope? **3.** To get the most out of 1 Peter, what will you put into it? How will you apply yourself to the group disciplines (of study, prayer, shared leadership, outreach, confidentiality, accountability, etc.)?

Notes

1:1-2 Peter begins his letter in the way most Greek letters began in the first century. He first identifies himself as the writer and then identifies those to whom his letter is written. He concludes the salutation with his own version of the standard Christian greeting: "Grace and peace be yours in abundance."

1:1 *Peter*. Peter was the leader of the 12 apostles. Before joining Jesus' band of disciples he was a fisherman on the Sea of Galilee. He worked with his brother Andrew in partnership with James and John (Lk 5:10). ***an apostle***. This means, literally, "one who is sent." It is the term used in the New Testament to identify those who were selected for the special task of founding and guiding the new church. To be an apostle one had to be a witness to the resurrection. ***God's elect***. To be "elect" is to be chosen by God to be a member of his family. Deuteronomy 7:6 expresses this: "The LORD your God has chosen you out of all the peoples on the face of the earth to be his people...." "The elect" had once been a phrase reserved for the nation of Israel, but after Jesus' death and resurrection it was used to refer to the Church. ***strangers in the world***. The Greek word used here is *parepidemoi*. It means "sojourner" and refers to those who are far from home, dwelling in a strange land. The term is used metaphorically for Christians, whose true home is in heaven. ***scattered***. The Greek word here is *diaspora*, which means "the dispersion." It originally referred to those Jews who were scattered in exile throughout a number of counties outside Palestine. Once again, Peter uses a term originally applied to Israel to refer to the Church. ***Pontus, Galatia, Cappadocia, Asia and Bithynia***. These are Roman provinces located in Asia Minor (now modern Turkey). The order in which they are named is the order in which a traveller would visit each.

1:2 Peter has already referred to the Christians as "God's elect." In this verse he points out the role of God the Father, God the Son, and God the Holy Spirit in the process of election. The doctrine of the Trinity emerged out of the experience of the people. ***chosen according to the foreknowledge of God the Father***. Israel knew itself to be chosen (selected, elected, picked) by God to be his people (Eze 20:5; Hos 11:1). They were to be the people through whom he would reveal himself to the rest of the world. The first Christians knew that they too had been chosen by God (See notes on 2:4 and 2:9). ***foreknowledge***. It is not just a matter of God knowing something before it happens. What God foreknows he brings to pass. Here his purpose is defined as "obedience to Jesus." ***the sanctifying work of the Spirit***. The choice of God takes effect by the work of the Holy Spirit. The aim of the work of the Spirit is holiness. The Holy Spirit awakens in people the longing for God, convicts them of their sin and opens them to the saving power of Jesus' death. Following conversion, the Spirit continues this sanctifying work by bringing power to overcome sin, assurance of sins forgiven, and new ways of living and feeling (the fruits of the Spirit). ***sanctifying***. To sanctify is to make holy. (The word "holiness" and the word "sanctification" both come from the same Greek root.) To be holy is not to be some sort of especially pious person (this is the common misunderstanding of the word). It is be set apart for God and thus to reflect his nature. ***for obedience to Jesus Christ***. The aim of this chosenness is obedience to Christ. The obedience referred to here is not the daily obedience of the believer. "It denotes his once-for-all obedience which led to his acceptance of reconciliation through the blood of Jesus Christ" (Best). ***sprinkling by his blood***. It is by means of the death of Christ that election is made possible. His death opened the way back to God. The image of sprinkling with blood comes from the Jewish sacrificial system. The primary Old Testament reference is to the acceptance of the covenant by the people of Israel (see Ex 24:1-8). God expressed his choice of Israel by means of a covenant in which he agreed to be their God and they agreed to obey him. Moses took half the blood of the sacrificial animals and sprinkled it on the altar and the other half on the people, thus sealing their commitment. ***Grace and peace***. At this point in a letter, the typical Greek writer would usually say simply: "Greetings." However, Peter and other New Testament writers (e.g Paul, see Php 1:2) christianized this statement. First, they transformed the Greek for "greetings" to "grace," a related word from the same Greek root. Then they added the Hebrew greeting "shalom," which in Greek became "peace."

UNIT 2   Praise to God for a Living Hope

1 Peter 1:3-12

Praise to God for a Living Hope

³Praise be to the God and Father of our Lord Jesus Christ!
In his great mercy he has given us new birth into a living hope
through the resurrection of Jesus Christ from the dead, ⁴and into
an inheritance that can never perish, spoil or fade—kept in
heaven for you, ⁵who through faith are shielded by God's power
until the coming of the salvation that is ready to be revealed in
the last time. ⁶In this you greatly rejoice, though now for a little
while you may have had to suffer grief in all kinds of trials.
⁷These have come so that your faith—of greater worth than
gold, which perishes even though refined by fire—may be
proved genuine and may result in praise, glory and honor when
Jesus Christ is revealed. ⁸Though you have not seen him, you
love him; and even though you do not see him now, you believe
in him and are filled with an inexpressible and glorious joy, ⁹for
you are receiving the goal of your faith, the salvation of your
souls.

¹⁰Concerning this salvation, the prophets, who spoke of the
grace that was to come to you, searched intently and with the
greatest care, ¹¹trying to find out the time and circumstances to
which the Spirit of Christ in them was pointing when he predicted the sufferings of Christ and the glories that would follow. ¹²It
was revealed to them that they were not serving themselves but
you, when they spoke of the things that have now been told you
by those who have preached the gospel to you by the Holy Spirit
sent from heaven. Even angels long to look into these things.

Questions

OPEN: 1. If you couldn't live in this
country, where would you choose to
live? Why? **2.** What in your family's
home would you like to inherit?

DIG: 1. What circumstances do you
think these people faced that caused
Peter to write like this? What is his
three-fold perspective on trials (vv.6-
7; see notes)? How do you account
for Peter's upbeat tone? **2.** What
work is each Person of the Trinity
doing in our lives? **3.** What basis for
a living hope does Peter give his
readers? **4.** What items here would
you list under "already available" to
a Christian (vv.6-9)? What would
you list under "not yet, but glad it's
coming" (vv.3-5)? How do the ones
on the "not yet" support the "already"
list? Are some on both lists? Why?
5. How does this salvation become
ours (vv.8-12)? What does this say
about how God chooses to reveal
himself, then and now?

REFLECT: 1. Imagine that your faith
is a mountain climb: What situations
in your life would be cliff-hangers?
Easy trails? Great views? Just walking up the path? What would you pull
out of your "1 Peter pack" in these
situations? **2.** What aspect of your
faith are you, like the prophets, struggling to know more about? **3.** Under
what fiery circumstances has your
faith become more genuine, by
melting it down to essentials?

Notes

1:3 *new birth*. When people encounter Jesus, something so radical happens that they can be said to be reborn into a whole new life. This no mere metaphor, but an accurate description of the transformation whereby a person becomes a part of the family of God and aware of spiritual reality. *a living hope*. This is the first thing new birth brings. Specifically here, their hope is that one day when Christ comes again, they will experience the full fruit of salvation when they experience the resurrection life of Jesus.

1:4 *inheritance*. New birth also brings a secure inheritance. To be born again means they have become part of a new family, and like all sons and daughters they can expect an inheritance. ***kept in heaven for you***. This inheritance is immune to disaster.

1:5 *shielded*. Not only is the inheritance guarded and immune to disaster, but so too are the Christians for whom it exists. ***salvation***. This is the object of the believers' hope and the content of their inheritance. The reference here is not to individual salvation, but to that moment in history when Christ will return again and all believers will come into the full enjoyment of eternity.

1:6 The experience of rebirth and the anticipation of an inheritance (both fruits of salvation) enable Christians to "exult with joy" despite trials and adversities. ***for a little while you may have to suffer***. By these two clauses, Peter gives perspective to their suffering. First, it will be temporary ("for a little while"). He may say this because he feels that the Lord's coming is near, or because in comparison with eternity what they are going through is but a moment. Second, such trials are circumstantial, perhaps even necessary ("you may have to" or "if need be"). Trials simply come. Certain circumstances make them inevitable. However, such trials do not fall outside God's providence. ***grief***. This stands in contrast to "rejoice." Within the trials there is both real grief and authentic rejoicing. ***trials***. Peter's first allusion to their persecution. The language indicates that he has in mind actual difficulties they have faced and are facing.

1:7 Peter adds a third perspective. They can endure because these trials will have a positive benefit. They will reveal the quality of their faith. ***gold***. Gold was the most precious of metals in the first century. Their faith is worth even more! ***fire***. Fire was used to burn away the impurities and so reveal the pure gold. In the same way, trials reveal the inner quality of faith. In an interesting twist, Peter notes that even though gold can stand up to fire, in the end it too, as part of the creation, will perish. ***proved genuine***. This will make evident the actual quality and strength of the faith they possess. Such trials do not create faith; they reveal what is already there.

1:10-12 The salvation that is still to come (vv. 3-5) and which is present even now (vv.6-9) was in the past the object of longing on the part of prophets (vv.10-12a) and even angels (v.12b).

1:11 *trying to find*. In the era preceding Jesus, there was frantic seeking to know what God would do. Even the OT prophets, as Peter points out here, had only a blurred vision of what was to come in God's grace. ***the Spirit of Christ***. The preexistent Christ was the one who inspired the prophets.

1:12 The Old Testament looked forward to the New. There is a continuity and a unity between both parts of the Bible. What the prophets predicted was preached by the apostles. ***It was revealed***. The process of revelation involves the searching and probing of prophets, coupled with and guided by the leading of the Spirit. In this way God reveals himself.

UNIT 3   Be Holy

1 Peter 1:13-2:3

Be Holy

¹³Therefore, prepare your minds for action; be self-controlled; set your hope fully on the grace to be given you when Jesus Christ is revealed. ¹⁴As obedient children, do not conform to the evil desires you had when you lived in ignorance. ¹⁵But just as he who called you is holy, so be holy in all you do; ¹⁶for it is written: "Be holy, because I am holy."ᵃ

¹⁷Since you call on a Father who judges each man's work impartially, live your lives as strangers here in reverent fear. ¹⁸For you know that it was not with perishable things such as silver or gold that you were redeemed from the empty way of life handed down to you from your forefathers, ¹⁹but with the precious blood of Christ, a lamb without blemish or defect. ²⁰He was chosen before the creation of the world, but was revealed in these last times for your sake. ²¹Through him you believe in God, who raised him from the dead and glorified him, and so your faith and hope are in God.

²²Now that you have purified yourselves by obeying the truth so that you have sincere love for your brothers, love one another deeply, from the heart.ᵇ ²³For you have been born again, not of perishable seed, but of imperishable, through the living and enduring word of God. ²⁴For,

> "All men are like grass,
>   and all their glory is like the flowers of the field;
> the grass withers and the flowers fall,
> 25   but the word of the Lord stands forever."ᶜ

And this is the word that was preached to you.

2 Therefore, rid yourselves of all malice and all deceit, hypocrisy, envy, and slander of every kind. ²Like newborn babies, crave pure spiritual milk, so that by it you may grow up in your salvation, ³now that you have tasted that the Lord is good.

Questions

OPEN: 1. What did you do as a child that got you into real trouble? **2.** What toy did you enjoy the most when you were younger? What happened to it? Would you play with it now if you had it? Be honest!

DIG: 1. From the five commands Peter gives in verses 13-15, how would you define "holy"? **2.** What reasons does Peter give for his commands (vv.17-21)? How can those reasons move us to obey? **3.** What does the OT imagery teach you about Jesus (vv.18-21; see notes)? **4.** Now that they have put their faith in Jesus, what difference will that make in the way these people think and act (1:22–2:3)?

REFLECT: 1. Are you more like a pilgrim, an explorer, or a landowner on this earth? Why? **2.** How does Peter's call to holiness challenge you in your life at home? Work? Community? Church? **3.** Judging by your time, effort, and money spent on each, which items come first— the perishable or "forever" ones? What attitudes or actions would Peter tell you to eliminate? How will you replace them with proper ones? **4.** In times of stress, what helps you to "set your hope fully on the grace of God," rather than to rely on your own wits to solve the problem?

ᵃ*16* Lev. 11:44,45; 19:2; 20:7   ᵇ*22* Some early manuscripts *from a pure heart*
ᶜ*25* Isaiah 40:6-8

Notes

1:13 *Therefore*. The salvation they have received results in a distinctive lifestyle involving clarity of mind, self-control, and an active hope. Given the severity of their situation, they cannot afford to act without thought, in an extreme or undisciplined way, or on the basis of despair.

1:14 *do not conform to the evil desires*. They are not to allow themselves to be shaped by the sensuality of their pre-Christian existence. They might be tempted to go along with the norms of others and so not stand out as different, thus escaping notice in the persecution. ***ignorance***. Not only was their pre-Christian life dominated by physical desires of all sorts, they also lived in ignorance of God. Pagans in the first century believed in God, but thought him to be unknowable and disinterested in human beings.

1:17 God is both their Father and their Judge. On both counts their attitude ought to be one of "reverent fear." ***strangers***. Christians are to make decisions not in terms of their present circumstances, but in the light of God's kingdom where their true home is found. ***reverent fear***. What Peter encourages here is not so much fear as it is awe.

1:18 *for you know that*. Peter is referring to what they knew from creeds, catechism, and liturgy. What Peter describes in the next few verses is the church's teaching on the redeeming work of Jesus. ***redeemed***. To redeem someone is to rescue that person from bondage. This is a technical term for the money paid to buy freedom for a slave.

1:19 The price of their ransom from their pagan lifestyle was not material ("silver and gold") but spiritual (the "blood of Jesus"). Here, Peter refers to Jesus in sacrificial terms as the innocent victim dying in place of others. ***blood***. In the OT, the blood of the sacrificial animal was offered to God in place of the life of the sinner. In the NT, it is not the sacrifice of animals that secures forgiveness; it is the death of Jesus who gave himself once for all. ***without blemish and defect***. Jesus was able to be such a sacrifice because he was without sin. This is a remarkable confession from one like Peter who lived in close contact with Jesus for three years. Of all people, Peter would have been able to point out sin in Jesus' life, had there been any.

1:21 *through him you believe in God*. Yet another aspect of Christ's work: they came to belief in the true and living God via Jesus. In Jesus they saw and understood who God was. ***raised him from the dead and glorified him***. Jesus' redemptive work began with the Cross, but was not complete until he was resurrected and glorified. Crucifixion, resurrection, and glorification are all part of one event. ***faith and hope***. Their faith (trust) and hope is that they, too, will share in the resurrection life of Jesus and in the glory that is his.

1:22 *purified/obeying*. Purification comes from obedience, and this issues in love for others. In the OT, there was a ritual purification of objects and people so as to fit them for the service of God (see Nu 8:21; 31:23). In the NT, purification is of a moral nature. Christians are called upon to rid themselves of those vices, passions, and negative attitudes (see 2:1) that make it difficult to love others. ***sincere love***. The word he uses for love is *philadelphia* (not *agape*) and refers to love between Christian brothers and sisters.

1:23-25 Peter contrasts human and divine birth (perishable seed vs. imperishable seed) in order to explain the origin of this new community.

2:1 They are to rid themselves of all those behaviors which work against brotherly love. The list Peter uses here is similar to other such vice lists in the NT (e.g., Ro 1:29–30; Eph 4:31). ***rid yourself***. This verb was used to describe taking off one's clothes. They must strip off, like spoiled and dirty clothes, their old lifestyle. ***hypocrisy, envy, and slander***. Specific vices that make relationships difficult. Hypocrites pretend to be one thing while, in fact, they are concealing their true motives. Envy is jealousy of another's place and privilege. Slander involves speaking evil of others when they are not there to defend themselves.

2:2 Having rid themselves of the old ways, they are like newborn babies. They need pure milk which will nourish them so that they grow to maturity. ***crave***. Having described them as newborn babies, he continues the metaphor by drawing upon the idea of the strong, natural, instinctual desire that infants have for milk. ***milk***. The word of God (see 1Co 3:2; Heb 5:12-14).

UNIT 4   The Living Stone and a Chosen People

1 Peter 2:4-12

The Living Stone and a Chosen People

[4]As you come to him, the living Stone—rejected by men but chosen by God and precious to him— [5]you also, like living stones, are being built into a spiritual house to be a holy priesthood, offering spiritual sacrifices acceptable to God through Jesus Christ. [6]For in Scripture it says:

> "See, I lay a stone in Zion,
>   a chosen and precious cornerstone,
> and the one who trusts in him
>   will never be put to shame."[d]

[7]Now to you who believe, this stone is precious. But to those who do not believe,

> "The stone the builders rejected
>   has become the capstone,"[e][f]

[8]and,

> "A stone that causes men to stumble
>   and a rock that makes them fall."[g]

They stumble because they disobey the message—which is also what they were destined for.

[9]But you are a chosen people, a royal priesthood, a holy nation, a people belonging to God, that you may declare the praises of him who called you out of darkness into his wonderful light. [10]Once you were not a people, but now you are the people of God; once you had not received mercy, but now you have received mercy.

[11]Dear friends, I urge you, as aliens and strangers in the world, to abstain from sinful desires, which war against your soul. [12]Live such good lives among the pagans that, though they accuse you of doing wrong, they may see your good deeds and glorify God on the day he visits us.

Questions

OPEN: What is your "dream house" like? Where would it be?

DIG: 1. What similarities does Peter show between Christ's experience and that of these people? **2.** How is Christ a cornerstone? How was this image used in the OT texts cited here (see notes)? **3.** Why would people stumble over the stone rather than build their lives on it? How are some attempts to build on it "acceptable" and beyond shame? **4.** How could you reword (in practical terms) what Peter meant by his pictures in verses 5 and 9? In what ways would it be difficult for Peter's readers to think of themselves in these terms? **5.** How is their new status with God to influence the way they live (vv.11-12)?

REFLECT: 1. If you were a war correspondent reporting from the front, how would you describe the war going on within yourself (v.11)? **2.** In what dark rooms of your life has God turned on a light? **3.** How do you respond to Peter's description of us as being chosen, a royal priesthood, and God's possession? When is it difficult to remember what God has made you? **4.** If you were to build a spiritual house from the living stones in your group, where would each member be positioned (walls, roof, telephone line, etc.) to realize his or her gifts? How does this fit who you are in Christ?

*6 Isaiah 28:16   *7 Or *cornerstone*   *7 Psalm 118:22   *8 Isaiah 8:14

Notes

2:3 In the end, however, it is not words about Christ that sustain them; it is Christ himself. They have "tasted that the Lord is good" (Ps 34:8).

2:4-12 Thus far Peter has pointed out two things about the identity of the people of God: (1) who they are is grounded in their experience of salvation (1:3-12), and (2) who they are is expressed in the kind of life they lead (1:13-2:3). Here he adds a third point: they have a special task. He uses two metaphors to describe this role: (1) they are *living stones* who are being built up into a spiritual house (2:4-8), and (2) they are a *royal priesthood* who declare the praises of God (2:9-12).

2:4 *the living Stone*. Peter shifts his description of Jesus from "the lamb without blemish" to "the living Stone." He gets this metaphor from two OT texts: Isaiah 28:16 (v.6) speaks of "a chosen and precious cornerstone" and Psalm 118:22 (v.7) speaks of the rejection of that stone. Both verses point out the supreme value of the cornerstone. Peter's point is that despite his rejection, Christ is the chosen one of God, and in the end he prevails. *living*. An allusion to Christ's resurrection (see 1:3,21). He is alive and able to give his resurrection life to those who come to him. *precious*. People may reject Jesus, but God gives him great honor.

2:5 *you also, like living stones*. So close is the relationship between Christians and Christ that Peter uses the same metaphor to describe both. The implication is that these Christians (like Christ) will know rejection and triumph. *being built into*. Stones by themselves, lying around on the ground, serve no function. But shaped together into a structure by a master builder, they become something of use and importance. *a spiritual house*. Peter shifts from a biological image ("born again") to an architectural one. The Church is the temple of God, made up of a close-knit community of men and women. Here is where God dwells, in contrast to temples built by human hands. *a holy priesthood*. Peter shifts the metaphor again. Not only are they a "spiritual house," they are the priests who serve in it! Priests were common figures in the first-century world. Their function was to mediate between God and the people. Typically, they were members of a special caste; priests were privileged and set

apart. But no such elitism exists in the Church. All Christians are members of this royal priesthood. *offering spiritual sacrifices*. The function of priests was to offer sacrifices of animals, grain, wine, etc. The sacrifice of Christians, however, is spiritual, not material, because Christ's great sacrifice of himself for the sins of the world was the ultimate and final sacrifice. What these NT priests can offer to God is love, faith, surrender, service, prayer, thanksgiving, sharing, etc. *acceptable to God through Jesus Christ*. All their efforts, however, would fail to satisfy God were it not for the sacrifice already made by Jesus himself.

2:6 In its original context, Isaiah was speaking to the leaders of Israel who had just made a pact with Egypt, in response to the threat of an invasion by Assyria. Isaiah points to the solid Temple as an illustration of where their true strength lies. They need to trust God, not alliances. Later rabbis understood this reference to the cornerstone to be a description of the Messiah whom God would establish in Zion.

2:7 In Psalm 118:22, the stone stood for Israel, which the world powers considered useless and which they threw away. However, God gave Israel the most important place in building his kingdom. This text was taken by the early church to be a prophecy of Jesus' rejection and death and his subsequent vindication (Ac 4:8-12). This interpretation came from Jesus, who spoke about himself in these terms (Mk 12:10).

2:8 *disobey*. Just as they are characterized by their "obedience to Jesus Christ" (1:2), others are characterized by disobedience. *destined for*. Those who have obeyed are chosen and destined for a glorious inheritance. Those who have stumbled over Christ have a different destiny.

2:9-10 In contrast to the destiny of their persecutors, they have a fine destiny. Peter lists a series of titles drawn from the OT (primarily from Isa 43:20-21 and Ex 19:5-6) which once were applied to Israel, but now belong to them.

2:11 *aliens and strangers*. They may be a chosen nation and a royal priesthood, but they are also outsiders in terms of the world in which they live.

UNIT 5   Submission to Rulers and Masters

1 Peter 2:13-25

Submission to Rulers and Masters

¹³Submit yourselves for the Lord's sake to every authority instituted among men: whether to the king, as the supreme authority, ¹⁴or to governors, who are sent by him to punish those who do wrong and to commend those who do right. ¹⁵For it is God's will that by doing good you should silence the ignorant talk of foolish men. ¹⁶Live as free men, but do not use your freedom as a cover-up for evil; live as servants of God. ¹⁷Show proper respect to everyone: Love the brotherhood of believers, fear God, honor the king.

¹⁸Slaves, submit yourselves to your masters with all respect, not only to those who are good and considerate, but also to those who are harsh. ¹⁹For it is commendable if a man bears up under the pain of unjust suffering because he is conscious of God. ²⁰But how is it to your credit if you receive a beating for doing wrong and endure it? But if you suffer for doing good and you endure it, this is commendable before God. ²¹To this you were called, because Christ suffered for you, leaving you an example, that you should follow in his steps.

²²"He committed no sin,
    and no deceit was found in his mouth."ᵏ

²³When they hurled their insults at him, he did not retaliate; when he suffered, he made no threats. Instead, he entrusted himself to him who judges justly. ²⁴He himself bore our sins in his body on the tree, so that we might die to sins and live for righteousness; by his wounds you have been healed. ²⁵For you were like sheep going astray, but now you have returned to the Shepherd and Overseer of your souls.

Questions

OPEN: When you were growing up, what authority figure was hard for you to respect? Why?

DIG: 1. With governmental persecution, why is submission to authority a concern for Peter (vv.12-14; see notes)? **2.** What does Peter mean by "submit" in this context? What equivalent verbs do you see here? **3.** How does their relationship with God influence their response to human authority? **4.** How can the suffering Christ (vv.21-25) help in situations far beyond our control? From these verses, how would you explain Christ's death to one unfamiliar with the Atonement?

REFLECT: 1. What "authorities" are over you? How do you apply verses 16-17 in those relationships? **2.** Peter wrote to a people who had no civil or employee rights. How would his advice be different to people in a country (or position) where their legal rights were being violated by authority gone bad (see Ac 16:35-37)? **3.** How could Jesus' example help when you face hardships you cannot change? How do you know when to submit to others voluntarily, and when it's right to resist them?

ᵏ22 Isaiah 53:9

18

Notes

2:13-25 In the first part of his letter, Peter deals with the *identity* of the people of God (1:1-2:12). In the second part, which begins with this unit, he looks at the *responsibilities* of the people of God (2:13-4:11). Here in this section, he begins his discussion of lifestyle by counseling them to adopt an attitude of respect. He starts by urging respect for everyone (2:13-17), with a special look at civil authorities. He then goes on to urge slaves to respect their masters (2:18-25), wives to respect their husbands (3:1-6) and husbands to respect their wives (3:7). He ends this section by reiterating his call for respect for everyone (3:8-12). Such an attitude, of course, would work to eliminate reasons for the persecution of Christians.

2:13 submit yourselves. This is the key concept in the next two units. What Peter urges is voluntary subordination in all spheres of human life. When the verb "submit" is used in the NT, it is voluntary in nature (e.g., "submit yourself"). The call is never to make others submit to you.

2:14 punish/commend. The role of these authorities is to prevent crime and suppress injustice. How they "commend those who do right" is not clear, though what Peter may mean by this is that governments tend to look with favor on law-abiding citizens (which is what Peter is urging these Asian Christians to be).

2:15 The Christians there were, apprarently, subject to slander ("ignorant talk") on the part of people who did not really know what was going on ("foolish men"). **ignorant talk**. The Greek word used here suggests willful ignorance; the unwillingness to find out what is really true.

2:16 Christ brought new freedom to men and women who had been long bound by rules and regulations. While affirming this new found freedom, Peter cautions that they must not let their liberty degenerate into license. **live as servants of God**. The paradox is that Christians are both free and bound. They are to "live as free men" while simultaneously they are "slaves of God" ("servants" is literally "slaves").

2:18 Slaves, submit yourselves. Slaves were the legal property of their masters. This fact, though inherently wrong, nevertheless defined the reality within which they had to live.

Peter (and other New Testament writers) does not counsel rebellion (it would have no chance of success at that point in history) or even "passive resistance" (which likewise would not work with masters who could, legally, take your life). What gave slaves the freedom to submit in this way is the sense that they as Christians were, in fact, members of a heavenly family and of a kingdom far more significant than the earthly reality within which they lived. Indeed, when the Lord returned (and they thought this would be quite soon), their true position would be revealed and they would live in this new reality for the age to come. **with all respect**. This phrase is literally, "with all fear." This is not, however, fear toward the master (Peter rejects such a posture in 3:14) but reverence toward God who is their true Master (see also v.21).

2:21-25 Jesus is their model for the way to act in the face of injustice. Here, Peter is probably quoting from (or alluding to) an ancient creed, hymn or liturgy. This whole section echoes Isaiah 52:13-53:12.

2:22 Peter directly quotes Isaiah 53:9 to point out once again the sinlessness of Jesus (see 1:19). A slave would understand that innocence was no guarantee of just treatment.

2:24 In a key passage about the atonement, Peter points out that Jesus was their representative. He bore their sins. He took upon himself the penalty which they deserved because of their sin. **so that**. Peter points to two results of Jesus' death on the cross: (1) because of it they are able to die to sin and (2) they can now live for righteousness. In other words, it is the moral impact of the Cross which Peter chooses to highlight here (and not the forgiveness of sin or remission of guilt which are also the result of the atonement). The death of Jesus makes it possible for them to leave their old lives of sin and follow instead a new way of life.

2:25 returned. They were once like lost sheep, but now they have been converted (i.e., they have turned around and come back to Christ). **Shepherd**. This was a common Old Testament image: God was like a Shepherd calling together his wandering sheep. In the New Testament this title was applied to Jesus.

UNIT 6   Wives and Husbands

1 Peter 3:1-7

Wives and Husbands

3 Wives, in the same way be submissive to your husbands so that, if any of them do not believe the word, they may be won over without words by the behavior of their wives, ²when they see the purity and reverence of your lives. ³Your beauty should not come from outward adornment, such as braided hair and the wearing of gold jewelry and fine clothes. ⁴Instead, it should be that of your inner self, the unfading beauty of a gentle and quiet spirit, which is of great worth in God's sight. ⁵For this is the way the holy women of the past who put their hope in God used to make themselves beautiful. They were submissive to their own husbands, ⁶like Sarah, who obeyed Abraham and called him her master. You are her daughters if you do what is right and do not give way to fear.

⁷Husbands, in the same way be considerate as you live with your wives, and treat them with respect as the weaker partner and as heirs with you of the gracious gift of life, so that nothing will hinder your prayers.

Questions

OPEN: As a child, how did you picture the man or woman of your dreams?

DIG: 1. How is the submission here similar in purpose to that in 2:13-15? What qualities are singled out? **2.** In what sense is Sarah a credible example? A humorous example (see notes)? **3.** How are husbands to live "in the same way" as their wives? **4.** How are verses 1 and 7 an example of applying 2:16 to marriage? What would you expect to see in a marriage built on mutual submission and servanthood?

REFLECT: 1. Married or not, what qualities here would you like to build into your relationships with the opposite sex? How would you put Peter's "beauty program" into practice? **2.** Does this passage advocate spouses staying in cruel situations? Why or why not?

Notes

3:1-7 Peter continues his discussion of relationships. His general principle is "respect for all," and thus far he has shown how this applies to the relationship between Christians and secular rulers and between Christian slaves and their masters. In this unit he looks at how wives and husbands are to relate to each other.

3:1 *wives*. The position of wives in first-century society was not dissimiliar to that of slaves. Under Jewish law a woman was a thing—she was owned by her husband in exactly the same way as he owned his sheep and his goats. Under no circumstances could she leave him, although he could dismiss her at any moment. Likewise, a woman had no rights under Roman law. She was completely subject to her husband. *in the same way*. By this phrase Peter makes a transition from slaves to wives. Just as the behavior of Christ was the model for slaves, so too is it for women. *be submissive*. Again, as he did for slaves, Peter counsels submission, not reaction or rebellion. Between Christian husbands and wives this was "mutual submission" as Paul made clear (Eph 5:21-33) and by definition mutual submission rules out hierarchial differences between spouses. But here Peter is thinking about marriage to a pagan husband who would consider himself in charge of his wife. *won over*. Peter (like Paul) does not counsel Christian women to leave pagan husbands. His desire is that the husbands be converted. So he describes the kind of attitude and behavior on the part of the wife that has the potential to lead an unbelieving husband to faith.

3:2 *purity and reverence*. What the pagan husband will notice about his wife is how she lives now that she has become a Christian. In particular, he will note her "purity." This word refers not just to sexual purity (chaste behavior) but also to purity of thought, motive, and action. He will see her "reverence" (i.e., that she has an awareness of God that causes her to live a good life).

3:6 *like Sarah*. The use of Sarah as an example of obedience shows that Peter was not devoid of a sense of humor. In Genesis, Abraham is shown as obeying Sarah as often as Sarah obeyed Abraham (see Gen 16:2,6;

21:11-12). The point of Peter's reference to Sarah is that wives in the new covenant can learn from their spirtual ancestress. If Sarah submitted in obedience, the least her spiritual daughters can do is to submit in servanthood. Sarah obeyed Abraham, but Christian wives, her spiritual daughters, are never told to "obey" their husbands neither here nor anywhere else in the Bible. Instead, they are asked to "do what is good." Sarah called Abraham "lord," but Christian wives are never told to call their husbands "lord" anywhere in the Bible. Instead, they are told to "let nothing terrify you" (v.6). "There is no fear in love, but perfect love casts out fear..." (1Jn 4:18) (Bilezikian).

3:7 In contrast to verses 1-2, where the focus is on Christian wives and pagan husbands, here Peter discusses how Christian husbands should relate to Christian wives. In the first century it was customary for the wife to adopt the religion of her husband so that if he were converted to Christianity, it is likely that she would be too. Peter seems to assume here that this would be the case. Peter reminds husbands that the respect they are to show to all people (2:17) is also due to their own wives. That a husband had any obligation to his wive was a startingly new principle in the first century. For example, the Roman writer Cato said: "If you were to catch your wife in an act of infidelity, you can kill her with impunity without a trial; but, if she were to catch you, she would not venture to touch you with her finger, and, indeed, she has no right." This, however, was not the Christian ethic. Both Peter and Paul make a point of identifying the obligations of a husband to a wife (see Eph 5:25-33). *be considerate*. That a husband should think about how he treated his wife (and not simply demand his "rights") was a new notion in a society where a wife was considered to be property. *treat them with respect*. This phrase is literally "assigning honor" and as such, is a paradoxial statement (in that inferiors give "honor" to superiors—in this Roman setting, women were unquestionalby the inferior party). *heirs with you*. Literally, joint-heirs or co-heirs. Both husband and wife are equal participants in the grace of God, again reinforcing the idea of the new mutuality that has come to men and women who are in Christ.

UNIT 7　Suffering for Doing Good

1 Peter 3:8-22

Suffering for Doing Good

⁸Finally, all of you, live in harmony with one another; be sympathetic, love as brothers, be compassionate and humble. ⁹Do not repay evil with evil or insult with insult, but with blessing, because to this you were called so that you may inherit a blessing. ¹⁰For,

> "Whoever would love life
> and see good days
> must keep his tongue from evil
> and his lips from deceitful speech.
> ¹¹He must turn from evil and do good;
> he must seek peace and pursue it.
> ¹²For the eyes of the Lord are on the righteous
> and his ears are attentive to their prayer,
> but the face of the Lord is against those who do evil."ⁱ

¹³Who is going to harm you if you are eager to do good? ¹⁴But even if you should suffer for what is right, you are blessed. "Do not fear what they fearʲ; do not be frightened."ᵏ ¹⁵But in your hearts set apart Christ as Lord. Always be prepared to give an answer to everyone who asks you to give the reason for the hope that you have. But do this with gentleness and respect, ¹⁶keeping a clear conscience, so that those who speak maliciously against your good behavior in Christ may be ashamed of their slander. ¹⁷It is better, if it is God's will, to suffer for doing good than for doing evil. ¹⁸For Christ died for sins once for all, the righteous for the unrighteous, to bring you to God. He was put to death in the body but made alive by the Spirit, ¹⁹through whomˡ also he went and preached to the spirits in prison ²⁰who disobeyed long ago when God waited patiently in the days of Noah while the ark was being built. In it only a few people, eight in all, were saved through water, ²¹and this water symbolizes baptism that now saves you also—not the removal of dirt from the body but the pledgeᵐ of a good conscience toward God. It saves you by the resurrection of Jesus Christ, ²²who has gone into heaven and is at God's right hand—with angels, authorities and powers in submission to him.

Questions

OPEN: How did you prepare for exams in high school: Regular study? All-night cramming? What, me worry? Wing it on "prayer"?

DIG: 1. How does the quote from Psalm 34 sum up what Peter has said in 2:11-3:9? What does he mean by setting apart Christ as Lord (v.15)? How will this affect their fears and hopes? **2.** What reasons for hope has Peter already given? **3.** What interpretation of verse 19 do you find most convincing (see also 4:6 and notes)? What does the Flood story add to your understanding of this difficult passage (vv.20-21 and notes)? **5.** What hope does Christ's life, death, and resurrection provide? How does the example of Christ's life give encouragement in times of suffering?

REFLECT: 1. Is your fellowship or church "in harmony" or "out of tune"? Why? What can you do to strengthen the harmony? How does your church exemplify the qualities of verse 8? **2.** What fears motivate people today? How does following Jesus as Lord free you from these fears? How would that free you to live differently? **3.** How does *hope* change your everyday behavior and cause people to ask about it? What situation seemed hopeless to you until God brought hope? **4.** Choose one difficult relationship in which you are currently involved. How could you *bless* (v.9) that person this week? What would you need to do?

ⁱ*12* Psalm 34:12-16　　ʲ*14* Or *not fear their threats*　　ᵏ*14* Isaiah 8:12
ˡ*18,19* Or *alive in the spirit,* ¹⁹*through which*　　ᵐ*21* Or *response*

Notes

3:8-12 Peter ends his comments (begun back in 2:13) with some general advice concerning how they are to relate to one another and to the pagan community.

3:9 Peter tells them not to retaliate against those who persecute them. ***blessing***. Instead, they are to bless their persecutors! This reinforces the advice he has given in the rest of this section. They are to act in unexpected ways.

3:10-12 Once again Peter refers back to Psalm 34 (see 2:3), where the theme is that the Lord will rescue his suffering children who trust in him.

3:13-17 Having pointed out how they are to relate to those who oppress them, now Peter looks directly at the oppression itself and how they are to respond to it. He reassures them that in the end, righteous behavior will be vindicated. Even if they are persecuted, they are not to fear. Instead, they must focus inwardly on Jesus while outwardly displaying good behavior.

3:14 ***But***. Peter does not mislead them, however. There is no assurance that good behavior will invariably shield them from harm. ***blessed***. If they do suffer, rather than being downcast, they are to count this as a privilege. ***do not fear***. The danger is fear.

3:15 ***But***. Instead of fear in their hearts, they need to place Jesus there. ***in your hearts***. At the core of their being Christ must reign. ***set apart Christ***. Lit., "sanctify" Christ. Christ is to be acknowledged as holy and worshiped as Lord. They are to open themselves to his inner presence. ***be prepared to give an answer***. Although this may refer to an official inquiry in which they are called upon to defend the fact that they are Christians, it probably is more general in reference. When anybody asks about the hope they have, they are to explain why they are followers of Jesus. ***the reason***. Greeks valued a logical, intelligent statement as to why one held certain beliefs.

3:16 This reply should be given not in a contentious or defensive way. ***a clear conscience***. The inner awareness of what is right morally. If they are living in the way Peter describes, they

will have nothing to hide; there will be no guilt to make them defensive.

3:18-22 The reason why they can be so confident in the face of suffering is because of the victory Christ has won over death. Furthermore, if they do suffer, they are simply walking the same path as their Lord.

3:18 ***died for sins***. Christ died—as have men and women down through the ages. But his death was different in that it was a full, sufficient, and adequate sacrifice that atones for the sins of all people. ***once for all***. The sacrifices in the temple had to be repeated over and over again; Christ's sacrifice was the final and perfect sacrifice through which all people in all ages find salvation. ***the righteous for the unrighteous***. His death was vicarious; i.e., he died in the place of others. ***bring you to God***. It is because of Christ's death that they are restored to a right relationship with God.

3:19 ***preached***. The nature of Jesus' proclamation has been interpreted as: (1) the gospel which is proclaimed to those who lived before Christ came, or as (2) the announcement to the rebellious spirits that their power has been broken. ***the spirits***. Who these spirits are is not clear. They have been variously identified as: (1) sinners who lived before the incarnation, or (2) the rebellious angels of Genesis 6:1-4. ***prison***. Likewise, the nature of this prison is not clear. It has been identified as: (1) hell, (2) a metaphor for the imprisonment that sin and ignorance brings, or (3) the world of spirits.

3:20-21 His next reference is to the Flood. Again, it is not clear what exactly Peter is saying. ***eight in all***. Noah and wife and their three sons (Shem, Ham, and Japhet) along with their wives. ***symbolizes***. Peter is using metaphors to explain spiritual truth. ***the pledge of a good conscience***. In baptism, they accepted the privileges and responsibilities of following Christ. ***saves you by the resurrection***. It is not the baptism in and of itself through which they found salvation. It is via Jesus they are saved. It is to the resurrected Jesus they pledge themselves. It is the resurrection life of Jesus which they experience.

UNIT 8   Living for God

1 Peter 4:1-11

Living for God

4 Therefore, since Christ suffered in his body, arm yourselves also with the same attitude, because he who has suffered in his body is done with sin. ²As a result, he does not live the rest of his earthly life for evil human desires, but rather for the will of God. ³For you have spent enough time in the past doing what pagans choose to do—living in debauchery, lust, drunkenness, orgies, carousing and detestable idolatry. ⁴They think it strange that you do not plunge with them into the same flood of dissipation, and they heap abuse on you. ⁵But they will have to give account to him who is ready to judge the living and the dead. ⁶For this is the reason the gospel was preached even to those who are now dead, so that they might be judged according to men in regard to the body, but live according to God in regard to the spirit.

⁷The end of all things is near. Therefore be clear minded and self-controlled so that you can pray. ⁸Above all, love each other deeply, because love covers over a multitude of sins. ⁹Offer hospitality to one another without grumbling. ¹⁰Each one should use whatever gift he has received to serve others, faithfully administering God's grace in its various forms. ¹¹If anyone speaks, he should do it as one speaking the very words of God. If anyone serves, he should do it with the strength God provides, so that in all things God may be praised through Jesus Christ. To him be the glory and the power for ever and ever. Amen.

Questions

OPEN: What did you do as a child or teenager that put you into a lot of trouble with mom or dad? Did you confess, or were you caught? (Or are you confessing for the first time now?)

DIG: 1. Imagine a specific, compromising situation that Peter's readers may have found themselves in: What would the pagans be saying to them? What does Peter tell them to think about in that situation? **2.** How are the realities of judgment (vv.5-7) and Christ's glory (v.11) to influence their daily behavior? **3.** What does this redemptive love look like in action (vv.8-11)? What role do the spiritual gifts mentioned here play? **4.** How would active love and these gifts of grace strengthen suffering people?

REFLECT: 1. Do you find that prayer leads to action, or that action leads to prayer? Conversely, what actions can hinder prayer? **2.** Which commands in verses 7-11 need your special attention this week? **3.** What is one gift you think each the member of your group has? How could that gift be used to show love?

Notes

4:1-6 A difficult passage to interpret correctly. However, it is clear that Peter is reassuring these Asian Christians that despite the suffering they face, they will prevail because of their identification in baptism with Jesus' death and resurrection.

4:1 *in his body*. A single Greek word which means lit., "in the flesh." It is repeated four times in verses 1-6. When it is first used ("Christ suffered in his body"), Peter probably has in mind the death of Christ. This also seems to be true when he says, "he who has suffered in his body is done with sin." Death is the only form of suffering that ends sinning permanently. In the case of Christ who was without sin, his death ended his identification with the sins of the world. Through his death he won a victory over sin on behalf of humanity (Stibbs).

4:4 Their pagan friends are astonished that they no longer lead this out-of-control lifestyle, but then their amazement turns into reaction and abuse.

4:5 This attitude will bring its own reward. These abusive pagans will themselves face judgment for their actions. *they will have to give account to him*. "Those who do not receive Him as their Saviour, must face Him as their Judge" (Stibbs). *the living and the dead*. The final judgment will include both those who are still alive when Christ returns and those who have already died. All will face judgment.

4:6 *the gospel was preached even to those who are now dead*. The meaning of this phrase has been much debated. It probably refers to those members of the church who heard and accepted the gospel but who have since died. Some scholars, however, connect this verse to 3:20-21 and conclude this is a reference to Christ's descent into hell, during which he proclaimed the gospel to those who were there. Some assert that those who heard Christ were those who lived prior to his coming and so never had a chance to hear the gospel. Others feel that all the dead get the chance to hear the gospel (and hence receive a second chance to come to faith). However, there is no necessary connection between 3:19-20 and 4:6; and in any case, the reference in 3:19 is to "spirits" while the reference here is to human beings who have died. *judged according to men in regard to the body*.

This phrase may mean that death itself is a form of judgment. The body dies because it is sinful.

4:7-11 Peter gives yet another reason for forsaking their old, self-indulgent lifestyle: history is about to end. This is the the time, he says, for self-discipline, prayer, and active love. In particular they must care for each other. Mutuality is the key: mutual love (v.8), mutual hospitality (v.9), and mutual ministry (vv.10-11).

4:7 *the end of all things*. The second coming of Jesus will mark the close of history when this world as it is now known passes away. *be clear minded and self-controlled*. As history draws to a close, their temptation might be to let their excitement get out of hand or to become self-indulgent. *so that you can pray*. When people are not thinking clearly or when their lives are out of control, they cannot pray properly.

4:8 Love is the key to a lifestyle of the last days. *love covers a multitude of sins*. A paraphrase of Proverbs 10:12. People tend to forgive those whom they love.

4:10 *gift*. This word is *charisma* and refers to the different gifts which the Holy Spirit gives to individual Christians for the sake of the whole body. *to serve others*. The point of these gifts is to use them for the sake of others. *God's grace in various forms*. Not all have the same gift. (See Ro 12:6-8; 1Co 12:7-10; Eph 4:11-12 for lists of various gifts.)

4:11 Peter discusses two gifts in particular: the gift of teaching and preaching and the gift of service. *if anyone speaks*. This is not the gift of tongues (ecstatic utterance, glossolalia) nor the gift of prophecy. The Greek word here refers to preaching and teaching. *as one speaking the very words of God*. Barclay paraphrases this: "If a man has the duty of preaching, let him preach not as a man offering his own opinions or propagating his own prejudices, but as a man with a message from God." *if anyone serves*. There are different kinds of service: helping those in need, giving leadership, providing money (see 1Co 12:5; Ac 6:1; Ro 12:13). *so that in all things God may be praised*. The purpose of these gifts is to glorify God through their exercise, not to bring glory to the one with the gift.

UNIT 9 Suffering for Being a Christian

1 Peter 4:12-19

Suffering for Being a Christian

[12]Dear friends, do not be surprised at the painful trial you are suffering, as though something strange were happening to you. [13]But rejoice that you participate in the sufferings of Christ, so that you may be overjoyed when his glory is revealed. [14]If you are insulted because of the name of Christ, you are blessed, for the Spirit of glory and of God rests on you. [15]If you suffer, it should not be as a murderer or thief or any other kind of criminal, or even as a meddler. [16]However, if you suffer as a Christian, do not be ashamed, but praise God that you bear that name. [17]For it is time for judgment to begin with the family of God; and if it begins with us, what will the outcome be for those who do not obey the gospel of God? [18]And,

> "If it is hard for the righteous to be saved,
>   what will become of the ungodly and the sinner?""

[19]So then, those who suffer according to God's will should commit themselves to their faithful Creator and continue to do good.

Questions

OPEN: What person or activity do you associate with *pain*?

DIG: 1. In what sense is the Christian's suffering part of Christ's suffering? Why should the Christian find joy in this? **2.** When Peter tells them to continue to do good (v.19), what reasons does he give?

REFLECT: 1. When you feel like giving up, what keeps you going? **2.** If you were asked to tell a group of new believers what to expect in the Christian life, what are some things (from 1 Peter) you would tell them? Why? **3.** We Christians are not persecuted a great deal by our government. What form, then, does your suffering for Christ take?

*18 Prov. 11:31

Notes

4:12-19 Peter now moves into the final section of his letter in which he addresses the challenge facing these Asian Christians. He does not introduce any new themes in this final section. Rather, he summarizes what he has already said in an intense and direct way as he encourages them to carry on in the face of suffering.

4:13 Rejoice. Rather than being bewildered ("surprised") at what is happening to them, they are actively to rejoice. They are not merely to passively endure these trials. They must come to understand them as a way to participate in the experience of their Lord. **participate**. In 2:20-21 Peter said that they were called to follow in Christ's footsteps. This they do when they suffer, even though they have only done what is good. In 4:1 he went a step further by reminding them that in their baptism they share in the death of Christ. Here he ties all this together by declaring that in this way they participate in the sufferings of Christ. **when his glory is revealed**. Peter has already reminded them that "the end of all things is near" (4:7). An awareness of this reality will enable them to cope with their suffering, not only because they know that their persecutors will one day have to answer to God for their deeds (4:5,17-18) but because at that point in time they will come into their share of the glory of Christ (see also 1:13).

4:14 glory. In the Old Testament, the primary meaning of this word (*kabod*) is that of weight and substance. A man of wealth is a man of substance, of *kabod*. His external appearance and bearing would, in nine cases out of ten, reflect his wealth, and also be called *kabod*. His wealth and dignity demanded and compelled respect and honor from his fellows, and this was called glory or honor. Hence weight, substance, wealth, dignity, noble bearing, and honor all contributed to its meaning. To these fundamental meanings Ezekiel added that of brightness. (Alan Richardson). This word came to describe the actual, visible radiance of God himself. Glory is not just what God reflects; it is who he is. So in other words, these Asian Christians will (and do) share in the very nature of God himself.

4:15 Not all suffering brings glory. Those that suffer because of wrongdoing do not gain this blessing. Peter's point (which he already made in 2:20) is that it is one thing to be punished for commiting a crime (which was not why these Asian Christians were being persecuted), and quite another to be punished for doing good (which is what was happening to them). **murderer/thief/criminal**. Each term connotes a recognizable form of wrongdoing which the civil authorities would clearly be justified in punishing (see 3:14). **meddler**. It is not clear to what this word refers. Some have translated it as "agitator" or "spy," implying revolutionary activity against Rome. But there is no evidence that this term even meant that. "We can only speculate what kind of meddling the writer has in mind (excessive zeal for making converts? causing discord in family or commerical life? over-eager denunciation of pagan habits? prying curiosity?), but [the author] plainly regards it as disreputable" (Kelly).

4:16 Christian. Apart from two references in Acts (11:26 and 26:28), this is the only other use of "Christian" in the New Testament.

4:17 it is time for judgment to begin with the family of God. It was understood that in the last days, the chosen people would suffer. This idea is found in the teaching of Jesus (Mk 13:8-13) and in the teaching of the apostles (1Co 9:31-32). In a sense, this is an encouraging sign. The tumultous End Times will precede the Second Coming, when it will be all over. When Christ returns, their inheritance and glory will begin. **what will the outcome be for those who do not obey the gospel of God?** The judgment will also reach out to those who disoby God. By implication, this judgment will be far worse (see also 2Th 1:5–10).

4:19 commit themselves. This is a technical term which refers to the act of depositing money with a trusted friend. This is the same word Jesus used in Luke 23:46: "Father, into your hands I commit my spirit." In the end it all comes down to this. Those who suffer for doing good, those who suffer only because they are Christians (v.16), must simply commit themselves to God. He is that trusted friend who can be relied upon absolutely to bear this trust. They will be safe with him.

UNIT 10   To Elders and Young Men/ Final Greetings

1 Peter 5:1-14

To Elders and Young Men

5 To the elders among you, I appeal as a fellow elder, a witness of Christ's sufferings and one who also will share in the glory to be revealed: ²Be shepherds of God's flock that is under your care, serving as overseers—not because you must, but because you are willing, as God wants you to be; not greedy for money, but eager to serve; ³not lording it over those entrusted to you, but being examples to the flock. ⁴And when the Chief Shepherd appears, you will receive the crown of glory that will never fade away.

⁵Young men, in the same way be submissive to those who are older. All of you, clothe yourselves with humility toward one another, because,

"God opposes the proud
but gives grace to the humble."ₒ

⁶Humble yourselves, therefore, under God's mighty hand, that he may lift you up in due time. ⁷Cast all your anxiety on him because he cares for you.

⁸Be self-controlled and alert. Your enemy the devil prowls around like a roaring lion looking for someone to devour. ⁹Resist him, standing firm in the faith, because you know that your brothers throughout the world are undergoing the same kind of sufferings.

¹⁰And the God of all grace, who called you to his eternal glory in Christ, after you have suffered a little while, will himself restore you and make you strong, firm and steadfast. ¹¹To him be the power for ever and ever. Amen.

[Scripture and questions continued on page 30]

Questions

OPEN: What is one of the most unruly groups you have had to "shepherd": Junior high kids on a school field trip? The church nursery during a long sermon? A small group that wouldn't cooperate? A meeting of professionals vying for recognition?

DIG: 1. What good and bad motives does Peter give for being in leadership? What qualities does he encourage elders to cultivate? Why would these qualities (and proper motivation) be important in times of persecution? **2.** What connections do you see between submissiveness, humility, and anxiety? What anxieties do these people face? What would replace their fears as they followed verses 6-7? **3.** What sources of opposition to the Christians has Peter spoken of already (see 2:12,13-14,18; 3:1,16; 4:3-4)? How do these relate to verse 8 here? What is the Christian's defense in this battle? The Christian's hope? **4.** Given that Babylon was one of the main enemies of Israel in the OT and that Peter is writing from Rome, what does he mean by verse 13? **5.** How do verses 10-13 sum up the pressures these believers were facing, as well as Peter's advice on this matter?

ₒ5 Prov. 3:34   ₚ12 Greek *Silvanus*, a variant of *Silas*

28

Notes

5:1-4 Peter has specific instructions for the leaders of the fellowship. It will not be easy for them to lead a church that is under fire.

5:1 elders. The leaders of the local congregation who probably functioned much in the same way as did the board of elders in a synagogue (i.e., they had administrative and spiritual responsibility for the congregation).

5:2 Be shepherds. This is a command. They cannot be passive or slack in what they do. They need to attend to their job of caring for God's people. **not because you must, but because you are willing**. The first of three antitheses by which he defines the spirit in which they are to hold this office. Here the contrast is between reluctant and willing service. **not greedy for money, but eager to serve**. The second antithesis: between service in order to profit financially, and service based on zeal for God. In all likelihood, elders received some financial remuneration (see 1Co 9:7-12; 1Ti 5:17-18). The temptation might be to regard their office simply as a job and not as a calling.

5:3 not lording it over those entrusted to you, but being examples. The third antithesis: between domineering those you are to care for, or coming to them in humility. **those entrusted to you**. This phrase probably refers to splitting up the flock into groups, each of which would be under the care of a particular elder.

5:4 Chief Shepherd. Peter has already described Jesus as the "Shepherd" (2:25). Here he adds an adjective that reminds the elders that their authority is not absolute, but derived from Jesus.

5:5 young men. The Greek social order was such that young men were considered subordinate to older men. **in the same way**. Probably a reference to 2:13-3:12, where he considered the question of how to relate to those who are above you in the social order. In that earlier section, the question was how to relate to those in secular society who have the potential to oppress you (rulers, slave owners, pagan husbands). Here the issue is how to relate to those in the church who are leaders. **be submissive**. Submission and respect are called for once again.

those who are older. This is the same word that is translated "elders" in verse 1. In fact, the elders (leaders) would most likely have been chosen from those who were older in age.

5:6 Humble yourselves. The same humility which is owed one another is owed God as well. **that he may lift you up in due time**. This will happen when Christ returns and they experience his glory.

5:7 Cast all your anxiety on him. This verb should be translated as a participle ("casting"), not as an imperative ("cast"), since in Greek it is connected to the imperative "humble yourself." It is not a separate commandment. "The true Christian attitude is not negative self-abandonment or resignation, but involves as the expression of one's self-humbling the positive entrusting of oneself and one's troubles to God" (Kelly).

5:8 Be self-controlled and alert. That they are not to be passive in the face of trouble is seen in this command. Coupled with conscious reliance on God, there must also be diligent effort on their part.

5:8b "The imminence of the End, prominent everywhere in the letter, is the backcloth of the scene. Christian apocalyptic, like Jewish, envisaged this as a period when the powers of evil would be particularly active and the elect would consequently be exposed to extraordinary trials (e.g., Mt 24:4-28; 2Th 2:3-12; 2Ti 3:1-9). The Asian Christians could observe the fulfillment of these terrifying surmises in the cruel treatment which seemed to descend so arbitrarily upon them and which, we may conjecture, tempted many of them to apostasy" (Kelly). **the devil**. Behind all their trials stands the Devil (*diabolos*). In the Old Testament he is known by the Hebrew name Satan. In the New Testament he is seen as the one who tempts (as he did with Jesus), as the prince of evil who rebelled against God, as the Antichrist, and as the one who seeks to undo God's purposes.

5:9 Resist him. Peter's advice is plain: do not run away, stand your ground and face him, refuse to give in to his purposes, trust in God (see also Eph 6:10-13; Jas 4:7; Rev 12:9-11). **your brothers throughout the world are**

[Notes continued on page 31]

1 Peter 5:1-14, continued

Questions

Final Greetings

[12]With the help of Silas,[p] whom I regard as a faithful brother, I have written to you briefly, encouraging you and testifying that this is the true grace of God. Stand fast in it.

[13]She who is in Babylon, chosen together with you, sends you her greetings, and so does my son Mark. [14]Greet one another with a kiss of love.

Peace to all of you who are in Christ.

REFLECT: 1. What area of your life would you like God to restore and make you strong, firm, and steadfast? 2. What leadership responsibilities do you have? (We all have some!) How do you score on Peter's leadership test? How can you improve your score? 3. In your life, where is "the lion" (v.8): (a) Just looking for you? (b) Nibbling at your heels? (c) Chewing you up? How can your group help you to resist him? What in this letter has helped? 4. What pictures of Christ has Peter drawn in this letter? How do those pictures bring peace (v.14) to you?

Notes, continued

undergoing the same kind of sufferings. Solidarity with Christian brothers and sisters around the world is a strong motivation for standing firm.

5:10-11 Satan may be their enemy and he is powerful and vicious ("like a roaring lion looking for someone to devour"), but he is no match for God. Assurance of strength and vic-tory is another motivation for continuing to resist evil.

5:12-13 Peter concludes his letter—as do most New Testament letters—with greetings and personal comments.

5:12 ***Silas***. Like Paul (and others), Peter used an amanuensis (secretary/scribe) to write this letter. In this case, Silas seems to have had an active part in shaping the final form of the letter with its rather polished Greek. The Silas referred to here is probably Paul's companion on his second missionary trip (Ac 15:40-18:5), a minister of the gospel (2Co 1:19), and the co-author with Paul of 1 and 2 Thessalonians. ***This is the true grace of God. Stand fast in it***. "The message of First Peter is that what the readers are experiencing is, in fact, the grace of God (cf. 1:13). In it they must stand" (Michaels).

5:13 ***She who is in Babylon...sends you her greetings***. Peter is (probably) referring to the church in Rome, where he was when he wrote this letter (see 2Jn 1,13). ***my son Mark***. Tradition has it that Mark was another of Peter's secretaries and in writing the Gospel that bears his name, Mark was expressing Peter's experience of Jesus. Certainly this phrase reflects a warm relationship between the two. ***a kiss of love***. At some point during the worship service, Christians would greet each other with an embrace, signifying their close bonds as brothers and sisters in the Lord. This was a ritual developed by the church (and not, as in so many other cases, adopted from Jewish liturgy).

ACKNOWLEDGMENTS

It is not possible to write notes such as these without building upon the work of many scholars. In fact, our role has been primarily that of "translators"—standing between the commentaries and technical literature on the one hand and the needs of lay Christians on the other hand. Ample use has been made of the usual research tools in the field of New Testament studies such as *A Greek-English Lexicon of the New Testament* (Bauer, Arndt & Gingrich), *Interpreter's Dictionary of the Bible*, *The New International Dictionary of New Testament Theology* (Colin Brown), *The Macmillian Bible Atlas* (Aharoni & Avi-Yonah), as well as other standard reference materials. In addition, use has been made of various commentaries. While it is not possible as we would desire, given the scope and aim of this book, to acknowledge in detail the input of each author, the source of direct quotes and special insights is identified. The original author's name is noted in the parenthesis that follows the citation. Bibliographical data is listed below.

There were three commentaries in particular that were especially useful in writing these notes. These are *The Letters of James and Peter* (The Daily Study Bible), William Barclay, Philadelphia: The Westminster Press, 1960; *A Commentary on the Epistles of Peter and Jude* (Thornapple Commentaries), J. N. D. Kelly, Grand Rapids, MI: Baker Book House, 1981 (first published in 1969) and *The First Epistle General of Peter* (Tyndale New Testament Commentaries), Alan M. Stibbs, London: The Tyndale Press, 1957.

The outline which was followed for 1 Peter is the work of J.Ramsey Michaels, formerly of Gordon–Conwell Theological Seminary (taken from a handout used in his 1980 class on 1 Peter). In seeking to understand what Peter was saying about marriage roles, use was made of *Beyond Sex Roles*, by Gilbert Bilezikian, (Grand Rapids, MI: Baker Book House, 1985).

Other commentaries that were referred to include: F.W. Beare, *The First Epistle of Peter* (3nd edition), Oxford 1970; Ernest Best, *1 Peter* (The New Century Bible Commentary), Grand Rapids, MI: Wm. Eerdmans Publishing Co.,1971; A.R.C. Leaney *The Letters of Peter and Jude* (The Cambridge Bible Commentary), Cambridge, England: Cambridge University Press, 1967; and Edward Gordon Selwyn, *The First Epistle of St. Peter* (Thornapple Commentaries), Grand Rapids, MI: Baker Book House, 1981.

TIME
FOR A
CHECK-UP

SEVEN COMMON SMALL GROUP AILMENTS AND HOW TO OVERCOME THEM

ARE YOU FEELING A LITTLE
NERVOUS ABOUT BEING IN A SMALL GROUP?

SYMPTOMS: Do you break out into a sweat at the mention of small groups. Does your mouth turn to sawdust when it comes "your turn" to share? To pray?

PRESCRIPTION: Take this test to see if you are ready to belong to a small group. If you answer "yes" on seven out of ten questions below, you are probably ready to take the plunge.

1. Are you looking for a place where you can deal with the serious questions in your life right now?   ☐ Yes   ☐ No

2. Are you open to the possibility that God has something special for your life?
   ☐ Yes   ☐ No

3. Are you open to the Bible as the source where God's will for your life can be explored?
   ☐ Yes   ☐ No

4. Are you able to admit that you do not have all the answers about the Bible? God? Your own life?   ☐ Yes   ☐ No

5. Are you able to let others have questions about the Bible or God?   ☐ Yes   ☐ No

6. Are you willing to accept people in the group that are "Prodigal Sons" and have a long way to go in their spiritual faith?   ☐ Yes   ☐ No

7. Are you willing to keep anything that is shared in this group in strict confidence?   ☐ Yes   ☐ No

8. Are you willing to share in the responsibility for the group and to support group members with your prayers?   ☐ Yes   ☐ No

9. Are you willing to give priority to this group for a short period of time (such as six to twelve weeks) and consider making a longer commitment after this time?
   ☐ Yes   ☐ No

10. Are you excited about the possibilities of belonging to a group that could make a difference in your life?   ☐ Yes   ☐ No

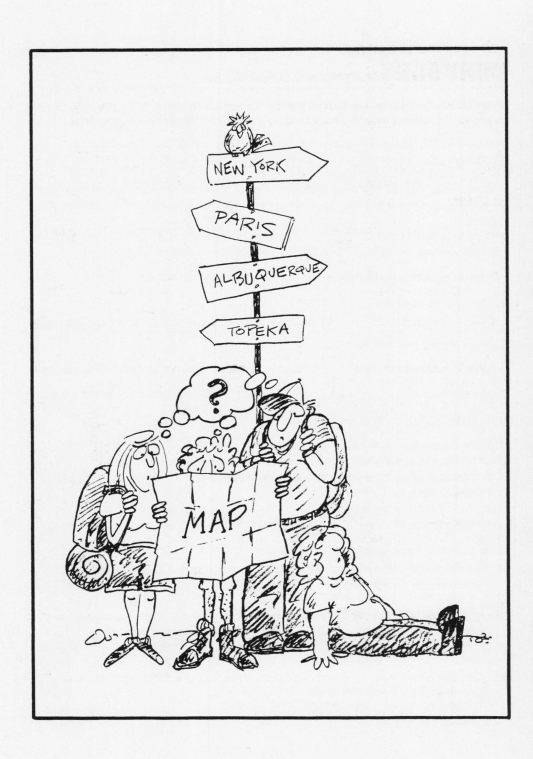

ARE YOU FEELING A LITTLE

CONFUSED ABOUT YOUR PURPOSE?

SYMPTOMS: Do you feel like you are playing on a team that doesn't have any rules? Any direction? Any idea of what you want to do or accomplish? Or where you are going?

PRESCRIPTION: Before you ever started the group, you should have decided on a COVENANT that spelled out your purpose, rules, expectations, etc. If you didn't, call "time out" and decide *together* on a covenant.

Here's how. Take the first sentence below and ask everyone to finish the sentence. Then, try to come up with a one sentence statement that you all can agree to. "The purpose of our group is . . ."

Then, take the second sentence and decide on your specific goals, etc. . . . until you have decided on your GROUP COVENANT. This becomes your game plan.

1. The purpose of our group is . . .

2. Our specific goals are . . .

3. We will meet _____ times, every _____ week, after which we will evaluate our group.

4. We will meet: Day of week _____ from _____ (time) to _____ .

5. We will meet at _____ , or rotate the place where we meet.

6. In addition to the study of the Bible, we will . . .

7. We will adhere to the following ground rules:
   - The leader of the group will be . . . or we will rotate the leadership.
   - The host for each meeting (other than the leader) will be . . . or we will rotate this responsibility.
   - Food/refreshments will be . . .
   - Baby-sitting, etc.

8. In addition to these general rules, we will agree to the following disciplines:
   - Attendance: To give priority to the group meetings
   - Participation: To share responsibility for the group
   - Confidentiality: To keep anything that is said strictly confidential
   - Accountability: To give permission to group members to hold you accountable for goals you set for yourself
   - Accessibility: To give one another the right to call upon you for help in time of need—even in the middle of the night.

C5

ARE YOU FEELING A LITTLE

DISTANT FROM THE OTHERS IN YOUR GROUP?

SYMPTOMS: Does your group start off like a Model A Ford on a cold morning? Or sag in the middle when you get to the Bible study? Do you find some of the people do all the talking . . . and others never get out of their "shell"?

PRESCRIPTION: Use the "flow questions" in the margin, next to the Scripture text, to guide the discussion. The questions are carefully designed to explode like time bombs on three levels of sharing: (1) OPEN—to break the ice, (2) DIG—to discuss the Scripture text, and (3) REFLECT—to take inventory of your own life.

OPEN/10-15 Minutes: ➤
Start off with a few good "stories" about your childhood or human-interest experiences. The better the "stories" at this level . . . the deeper the group will share at the close. (There is a close parallel between "childlikeness" and "Christlikeness".

> OPEN: 1. When you were growing up, who were the people you were told not to associate with?What part of the city or country would you be warned about? What would have happened if you had gone there? 2. Where was the "watering hole" in your home town, where everybody went to "hang out"?

DIG/30-45 Minutes: ➤
You read the Scripture text at this point and go around on the first question . . . looking to the text for your answers. The questions are designed to force the group into observation/interpretation. (This is called the "inductive method" to Bible study). By the way, you do not have to finish all the questions. Save time at the close for Reflect.

> DIG: 1. From 1:19-28 and 3:22-26, why might Jesus decide to "get out of town" in a hurry? 2. As someone taught from birth to despise the Samaritans, how would you feel when Jesus decided to go through Samaria instead of the long way home? 3. Since "nice" girls did not come to the water well at noontime ("the sixth hour"), why do think Jesus risked his reputation to ask a favor of this woman? 4. How would

REFLECT/15-30 Minutes: ➤
This is the heart of the Bible study. The purpose is to take inventory of your own life and share with the group "what God is telling you to do." The questions are "high risk"; that is, the group is asked to share on a "need level", before moving on to prayer.

> REFLECT: 1. What social, ethnic, or religious barriers are difficult for you to break through? How would Jesus relate to these people you find difficult? 2. What aspects of Jesus' conversation could you use as a model for your own discussions with searching friends?

FLOW QUESTIONS/DISCLOSURE SCALE

At the beginning of the meeting: Ice breaker questions.	In the middle of the meeting: Bible search questions.	At the close of the meeting: Personal inventory.
LOW RISK	MODERATE RISK	HIGH RISK

Philippians 1:3-11

Thanksgiving and Prayer

³I thank my God every time I remember you. ⁴In all my prayers for all of you, I always pray with joy ⁵because of your partnership in the gospel from the first day until now, ⁶being confident of this, that he who began a good work in you will carry it on to completion until the day of Christ Jesus.

⁷It is right for me to feel this way about all of you, since I have you in my heart; for whether I am in chains or defending and confirming the gospel, all of you share in God's grace with me. ⁸God can testify how I long for all of you with the affection of Christ Jesus.

⁹And this is my prayer: that your love may abound more and more in knowledge and depth of insight, ¹⁰so that you may be

Questions

OPEN: When you care for someone, are you more likely to send a funny card or a touching one? What card still brings back a smile (or a warm fuzzy) for you?

DIG: 1. What are Paul's feelings for this church? What does that show about his leadership style? **2.** What is the "good work" to be completed (v.6)? How so (see 2:12-13)? **3.** What qualities are key to a fellowship (vv.9-11)?

REFLECT: What concerns for your group does Paul's prayer bring to mind? Paraphrase and personalize Paul's prayer to make it your own.

ARE YOU FEELING A LITTLE
INTIMIDATED BY THE BIBLE SCHOLARS IN YOUR GROUP?

SYMPTOMS: Are you afraid that your ignorance about the Bible could be embarrassing? For instance: if someone asked you who Melchizedek was, what would you say? If you said "an old linebacker for the Raiders", you would be wrong. Twice wrong.

PRESCRIPTION: Don't despair. Most of the people in your group don't know either. And that's O.K. This Bible study group is for BEGINNERS. And for BEGINNERS, there are Notes on the opposite page to help you keep up to speed with the rest of the group.

NOTES include:

- ☐ Definitions of significant words.

- ☐ Historical background: the political, social, economic context behind the words in the text.

- ☐ Geographical setting: facts about the country, terrain, lakes, crops, roads, and religious shrines.

- ☐ Cultural perspective: lifestyles, homes, customs, holidays, traditions, and social patterns.

- ☐ Archeological evidence: recent findings that sheds light on the Bible events.

- ☐ Summary/Commentary: recap of the argument to keep the passage in the context of the whole book.

Notes

1:3 *every time I remember you*. This is a difficult phrase to translate from the Greek. What it seems to mean is that during his times of prayer, Paul "was compelled by love to mention his Philippian friends. This means, then, that Paul gave thanks not whenever he happened to remember them, but that he regularly gave thanks for them and mentioned them to God at set times of prayer" (Hawthorne).

1:4 *with joy*. "Joy" is a theme that pervades Philippians. This is the first of some fourteen times that Paul will use the word in this epistle. He mentions "joy" more often in this short epistle

confirming the gospel. These are legal terms. The reference is to Paul's defense before the Roman court, in which he hopes to be able not only to vindicate himself and the gospel from false charges, but to proclaim the gospel in life-changing power to those in the courtroom. (See Ac 26 for an example of how Paul did this when he stood in court before Agrippa and Festus.)

1:8 *I long*. Yet another word characteristic of Paul. He uses it seven of the nine times it is found in the New Testament. This is a strong word and expresses the depth of Paul's feelings for them, his desire to be with them, and the wish to minister

ARE YOU FEELING A LITTLE
TEMPTED TO KEEP THE GROUP JUST FOR YOURSELF?

SYMPTOMS: Two feelings surface: (1) if we let anyone into our group, it would destroy our "closeness", and/or (2) if we let anyone into our group, we would not have time enough to share.

PRESCRIPTION: Study the ministry of Jesus and the early church: the need for "closeness" and the danger of "closedness." How did Jesus respond to his own disciples when they asked to "stay together" and build a "monument." Note the Story of the Transfiguration in Mark 9:2–13.

SOLUTION #1: Pull up an empty chair during the prayer time at the close of the group and pray that God will "fill the chair" with someone by the next week.

SOLUTION #2: When the group reaches seven or eight in number, divide into two groups of 4—4 at the dining table, 4 at the kitchen table—when the time comes for the Bible study . . . and reshuffle the foursomes every week so that you keep the whole group intact, but sub-group for the discussion time.

THREE PART AGENDA FOR GROUP USING THE SUB-GROUP MODEL

GATHERING/15 Minutes/All Together.
Refreshments are served as the group gathers and assignments are made to sub-groups of 4.

SHARING/30–45 Minutes/Groups of 4.
Sub-groups are formed to discuss the questions in the margin of the text.

CARING/15–30 Minutes/All Together.
Regather the whole group to share prayer requests and pray.

ARE YOU FEELING A LITTLE

BORED WITH YOUR BIBLE STUDY GROUP?

SYMPTOMS: You feel "tired" before the meeting starts. And worse after it is over. The sharing is mostly a "head-trip". One person is absent three weeks in a row. Another is chronically late. You feel like your time could be better spent doing something else, but you don't know how to say it.

PRESCRIPTION: You may be having a group "mid-life" crisis. Here are three suggestions.

1. Call "time out" for a session and evaluate your Covenant (page 5). Are you focused on your "purpose"? Your goals? Are you sticking to your rules? Should you throw out some of your rules? (Nobody said you can't.)

2. Check to see if your group is hitting on all three cylinders for a healthy small group. (1) Nurture/Bible Study, (2) Support for one another, and (3) Mission/Task. Here's a way to test yourself.

   On a scale from 1 to 10, circle a number to indicate how you feel your group is doing on each of these three cylinders.

   ON NURTURE/BIBLE STUDY: Getting to know the Bible. Letting God speak to you about His plans for your life through the Scripture.

We're doing a LOUSY JOB	1	2	3	4	5	6	7	8	9	10	We're doing a GREAT JOB

   ON SUPPORT: Getting to know each other. Caring about each other. Holding each other accountable for the best God has for you.

We're doing a LOUSY JOB	1	2	3	4	5	6	7	8	9	10	We're doing a GREAT JOB

   ON MISSION/TASK: Reaching out to others in need. Drawing people into the group, or sponsoring another group.

We're doing a LOUSY JOB	1	2	3	4	5	6	7	8	9	10	We're doing a GREAT JOB

3. Consider the possibility that God is saying it is time to shut down the group. Take time for a party. Give everyone a chance to share what the group has meant to him/her and what he/she will remember most about the group.

ARE YOU FEELING A LITTLE

ITCHY ABOUT DOING SOMETHING MORE?

SYMPTOMS: You're feeling tired of just sitting around studying the Bible. You have friends who are really hurting. Struggling. God seems to be saying something, but you don't know just what.

PRESCRIPTION: Consider the possibility that God is asking your group to split up and give birth to some new groups. Here are some steps:

1. Brainstorm together. Go around and have everyone finish the first sentence below. Then, go around on the second sentence, etc.

   I am concerned about a group for . . . (such as . . . "a group for young mothers, single parents, blended families, parents of adolescents, men at my office, young couples, empty nesters . . ." etc.).

   I wish we could . . .

   I would be willing to . . .

2. Make a list of prospects (people from the fringe of the church or outside of any church) that you would like to invite to a dinner party at which you could explain "what this Bible study group has meant to you."

3. Write each of these people a hand-written invitation on your personal stationary, inviting them to the dinner party at your home. (Don't bother to use the church bulletin. Nobody reads that.)

HOW TO TURN YOUR GROUP INTO A MISSIONARY GROUP

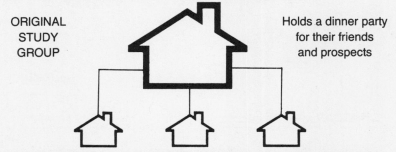

ORIGINAL
STUDY
GROUP

Holds a dinner party
for their friends
and prospects

NEW STUDY GROUPS ARE FORMED/ORIGINAL GROUP THE LEADERS

(P.S. You can still get back together with the whole group once a month for a "reunion" to share exciting "stories" of your new groups.

Introduction to
JAMES

Authorship

In the New Testament, there are apparently five men by the name of James, but only two who might conceivably have written this epistle—either James the apostle, or James the Just, the half-brother of Jesus. Since it is almost certain that James the apostle (the son of Zebedee) was killed by Herod in A.D. 44 (before the epistle could have been written), traditionally the author has been assumed to be James, the leader of the church in Jerusalem and the brother of Jesus (Mk 6:3).

The pilgrimage of James to faith is fascinating. At first Jesus's family was hostile to his ministry (Jn 7:5) and, in fact, tried to stop it at one point (Mk 3:21). Yet after Jesus' ascension, Jesus' mother and brothers are listed among the early believers (Ac 1:14). For James, this coming to faith may have resulted from Jesus' postresurrection appearance to him (1Co 15:7).

Apart from the fact that they were closely related, James' relationship to Jesus is not totally clear. Some maintained that they were cousins (the New Testament word for "brother" is looser in meaning than the modern equivalent). Some suggest he was a half-brother to Jesus, a son of Mary and Joseph. Others say that James might have been an older stepbrother of Jesus by a (conjectural) marriage of Joseph previous to his marriage to Mary. The latter view (which excludes any blood relationship to Jesus), might better explain the failure of Jesus' brother to believe in him during his lifetime (Mk 3:21, Jn 7:2-8). And a lack of concern for Mary (because she was only their stepmother) might also explain why Jesus, from the cross, committed his mother to the apostle John (Jn 19:25-27). But the reason may have been that Mary's discipleship alienated her from her other children, who still did not believe in Jesus (Robert H. Gundry, *A Survey of the New Testament*, p. 324).

A Church Leader

In any case, James emerged as the leader of the church in Jerusalem. It was to James that Peter reported after his miraculous escape from Herod's prison (Ac 12:17). James presided over the first Jerusalem Council, which decided the important question of whether to admit Gentiles to the church (Ac 15, especially vv. 13-21). James was consulted by Paul during his first trip to Jerusalem after his conversion (Gal 1:19), and then James joined in the official recognition of Paul's call as Apostle to the Gentiles (Gal 2:8-10). It is to James that Paul later brought the collection for the poor (Ac 21:17-25).

A Jew

We also know that James was a strict Jew who adhered to the Mosaic Law (Gal 2:12), yet unlike the Judaizers, he supported Paul's ministry to the Gentiles (Ac 21:17-26). Later accounts indicate that James was martyred in A.D. 62.

The question of who wrote the book of James is still, however, somewhat of a puzzle, primarily because Jesus and his saving work is mentioned so little—a curious omission if the author was Jesus' brother. This question baffled even the ancient church. Both the Latin Father Jerome and the church historian Eusebius (as well as others) observe that not all accept James as having been written by our Lord's brother.

Audience

James is one of the Catholic (or general) Epistles (along with 1 and 2 Peter, John's epistles, and Jude), so called because it has no single destination. Thus it is not clear to whom James is addressing his comments. At first glance, it appears that he is writing to Jewish Christians dispersed around the Greek world: "to the twelve tribes scattered among the nations" (1:1). But since Peter uses the same sort of inscription (1Pe 1:1-2) when he is clearly addressing

Gentile Christians (who consider themselves the new Israel), James' destination remains unclear. In fact, a strong case can be made (see Sophie Laws, *The Epistle of James: Harper New Testament Commentaries*, pp. 32-38) that James was writing for a community of "God-fearers," that is, Gentiles who had been deeply attracted to Judaism. That such folk were then drawn to Christianity is clear from examples in Acts, such as Cornelius (Ac 10:2, 22), Lydia (Ac 16:14), Titius Justus (Ac 18:7), and others. This would help to explain the convergence of Jewish, Greek, and Christian elements in the book of James.

Date

It is difficult to date the book of James. Some place it very early, around A.D. 45, making it the first New Testament book. Others date it quite late.

Characteristics

Among the New Testament books, James is an oddity. It is written in quite a different style from the others, more like the book of Proverbs than Paul's epistles. But even more than its style, its contents set James apart. It does not treat many of those themes we have come to expect in the New Testament.

Its Omissions

There is no mention of the Holy Spirit, and no reference to the redemptive work or resurrection of Christ. In fact, it contains only two references to the name Jesus Christ (1:1 and 2:1). Furthermore, when examples are given, they are drawn from the lives of Old Testament prophets, not from the experiences of Jesus. Although the title *Lord* appears eleven times, it generally refers to the name of God and not to Jesus. Indeed, it is God the Father who is the focus in the book of James.

Thus, Martin Luther wrote in his preface to the New Testament that "St. John's Gospel and his first epistle, St. Paul's epistles, especially Romans, Galatians, and Ephesians, and St. Peter's first epistle are the books that show Christ and teach you all that is necessary and salvatory for you to know, even if you were never to see or hear any other book or doctrine. Therefore St. James's epistle is really an epistle of straw, compared to these others, for it has nothing of the nature of the gospel about it."

Its Contributions

Luther notwithstanding, James is clearly a Christian piece of writing. Full of wisdom, it is based solidly on the teachings of Jesus and is a genuine product of first-century Christianity. To be sure, it is not as directly theological as many other New Testament Epistles, but then James' concern is not doctrinal (which he seems to assume) but rather ethical —how the Christian faith is to be lived on a day-by-day basis. As Johann Gottfrieds Herder wrote, "If the Epistle is of straw, then there is within that straw a very hearty, firm, nourishing...grain" (*Briefe Zweener Brüder Jesu in unserem Kanon*, in *Herders sömmtliche Werke* ed. Bernard Suphan, Vol 7, p. 500, n.2).

Background

James draws his language, images, and ideas from three worlds: Judaism, Greek culture, and early Christianity. From Christianity, he uses the language of eschatology (5:7-9), common patterns of Christian ethical instructions which parallel those of 1 Peter (1:2-4,21; 4:7-10) and echo the teachings of Jesus (e.g., 1:5, 17; 2:5, 8, 19; 4:3; 5:12). From Judaism, he draws his insistence on the unity of God, concern for keeping the law, and quotations from Jewish Scriptures (2:8,11,21-25; 4:6; 5:11,17-18) along with the use of certain Jewish terms (e.g., the word translated "hell" in 3:6 is the Hebrew *Gehenna*). Christianity and Judaism shared his concern for the poor and oppressed. From the Greek-speaking world —"the shared culture of the eastern Mediterranean area within the Roman Empire that resulted from the conquests of Alexander the Great" (Laws, *The Epistle of James,* p.5)—he takes the language (which he uses with skill), the source of his Old Testament quotations (he uses the Greek Old Testament, not the Hebrew version), Greek forms of composition, and metaphors drawn from Greek and Latin sources (e.g., the horse and the ship in 3:3-4).

Structure

Written in epistle (letter) form, James is loosely structured and rambling in style. It seems to jump from one idea to another without any overall plan, apart from that of providing a manual of Christian conduct. In fact, the book of James shares many characteristics of the sermonic style of both Greek philosophers and Jewish rabbis. As in Greek sermons, James carries on a conversation with a hypothetical opponent (2:18-26; 5:13-16), switches subjects by imperatives, relies on vivid images from everyday life (3:3-6; 5:7), illustrates points by reference to famous people (2:21-23,25; 5:11,17), uses vivid antitheses in which the right way is set alongside the wrong way (2:13,26), begins the sermon with a striking paradox that captures the hearers' attention (1:2, "consider it pure joy...whenever you face trials"), is quite stern (2:20; 4:4), and clinches a point by means of a quotation (1:11,17; 4:6; 5:11,20) (Ropes and Barclay). It should be noted, as William Barclay writes:

> The main aim of these ancient preachers, it must be remembered, was not to investigate new truth; it was to awaken sinners to the error of their ways, and to compel them to see truths which they knew but deliberately neglected or had forgotten (*The Letters of James and Peter,* pp. 33-34).

Jewish sermons had many of the same characteristics. But rabbis also had the habit, as did James, of constructing sermons that were deliberately disconnected—a series of moral truths and exhortations, strung together like beads.

Theme

While James clearly stands in the tradition of other Christian writers, he has some special concerns. The relationship between rich and poor crops up at various points (1:9-11; 5:1-4)— an issue of special significance to the modern affluent West. He is concerned about the use and abuse of speech (1:19,22-24, 26; 2:12; 3:3-12; 5:12). He gives instruction on prayer (1:5-8; 4:2-3; 5:13-18). Above all, he is concerned with ethical behavior. How believers act, he says, has eschatological significance—future reward or punishment depends on it. In this regard, James bemoans the inconsistence of human behavior (1:6-8,22-24; 2:14-17; 4:1, 3). Human beings are "double-minded" (1:8; 4:8), in sharp contrast to God, who is one (2:19).

James has been incorrectly understood by some to be contradicting Paul's doctrine of justification by faith (2:14-26). In fact, if James had Paul in mind at all, he was addressing himself to those who had perverted Paul's message—insisting that it doesn't matter what you do, as long as you have faith. James responded by asserting that works are the outward evidence of inner faith. Works make faith visible to others. In contrast, Paul was concerned with our standing before God. As is evident from Romans 12-15, Paul certainly agreed with James that faith in Christ has direct implications for how believers live.

UNIT 1   Salutation

James 1:1

1 James, a servant of God and of the Lord Jesus Christ,
To the twelve tribes scattered among the nations:

Greetings.

Questions

OPEN: 1. When you were young, who was the adult that most often gave you advice about growing up? How did you feel when that person wanted to sit down and talk with you? **2.** What is one piece of wisdom that this person gave you that you still recall? That you still practice?

DIG: Read the Introduction and leaf through James. Note captions and other clues about the book's meaning. **1.** From what you observed in your "leafing" and the Introduction, what are some of the things to look for in this book? What are your first impressions? What are the key ideas? The common refrains? **2.** Select someone in the group to act as scribe. Have him or her write out on a big sheet of paper each of the issues which the group identifies in the book. What expectations does this list create regarding what you will learn from studying James? **3.** Since there is so little doctrinal teaching in this letter, what does that tell you about the readers? About James? About the Christian life? **4.** If James were dropped from the Bible, what would be missing from the story of God's redemptive work in history?

REFLECT: 1. Looking at the list of issues that James addresses, which one strikes you as an area in which you would like to grow? Why? How do you expect this letter to challenge you? How can we help one another meet these challenges and make the changes James requires of us? **2.** Some groups evaluate a person's spiritual maturity by what that person *believes*, while others do so by what that person *does*. What are the values and limits of each approach? Which do you tend to use? How do you feel about using the second approach as a way to evaluate your life during the group study of James? **3.** To get the most out of James, what will you put into it? How will you apply yourself to the group disciplines (of study, prayer, shared leadership, outreach, confidentiality, accountability, etc.)?

Notes

1:1 James begins his letter in the same way most Greek letters began—by naming the sender and the recipient and then by offering a greeting. This is a letter *from* James the brother of Jesus (he is so well-known that he does not need further identification) *to* Jewish Christians living outside the region of Palestine. **James**. "James" is the Greek version of the common Hebrew name "Jacob." As discussed in the Introduction, it refers to the brother of Jesus who was known in the early church as "James the Just." The pilgrimage of James to faith is fascinating. At first, the family of Jesus, presumably including James, was hostile to Jesus' ministry (Jn 7:5) and, in fact, tried to stop it at one point (Mk 3:21). Yet following Jesus' ascension, Jesus' mother and brothers are listed among the early believers (Ac 1:14). For James, this coming to faith may have resulted from Jesus' postresurrection appearance to him (1Cor 15:7). In any case, James emerges as the leader of the church in Jerusalem. It is to James that Peter reports after his miraculous escape from Herod's prison (Ac 12:17). It is James who presides over the first Jerusalem Council in which the important question is decided on whether to admit Gentiles to the Church (Ac 15, esp. vv.13-21). James is consulted by Paul during his first trip to Jerusalem (Gal 1:19). Later, James joins in the official recognition of Paul's call as apostle to the Gentiles (Gal 2:8-10). It is to James that Paul brings the collection for the poor (Ac 21:17-19). We also know that James was a strict Jew, adhering to Mosaic Law (Gal 2:12). Yet he did back Paul's ministry to the Gentiles (Ac 21:17-26), unlike the Judaisers. Extra-biblical accounts tell us that James was martyred in A.D. 62. The high priest Annas the Younger seized James, who was then condemned and stoned to death. A few years later, in A.D. 66, the church in Jerusalem (which James headed) itself came to an end. Fearing the approaching Roman armies, the church members fled to Pella in the Transjordan and never returned to Jerusalem. **a servant**. James is so well-known that he needs no further designation. In fact, in the Letter of Jude this wide recognition of James is used by the author to identify himself: "Jude, a servant of Jesus Christ and *a brother of James*." (In contrast, it is often necessary for Paul to identify himself as an apostle, thereby asserting his apostolic authority in the matters about which he is writing. James' modest designation of himself as "a servant" instead of "Bishop of Jerusalem" or "the brother of Jesus" is probably a reflection of his genuine humility. Here he identifies Jesus as the "Lord" (master), therefore the appropriate relationship of all others to Jesus is as *servants* (literally "slaves"). **the twelve tribes**. This is a term used in the Old Testament to refer to the nation of Israel, even after ten of the twelve tribes were lost and never reconstituted following Israel's captivity by the Assyrians. In the New Testament, it came to be associated with the Christian church. Christians saw themselves as the new Israel (Rm 4; 9:24-26; Php 3:3; 1Pet 2:9-10) **scattered.** The word is, literally, *diaspora* and was used by Jews to refer to those of their number living outside Palestine in the Gentile world. Here it probably refers to those Jewish Christians living outside Palestine (see 1Pet 1:1). **Greetings**. The Greek word used here, *chairein*, is unusual for the New Testament (though it is the standard salutation used in secular Greek letters). Other writers generally "Christianize" the greeting.

UNIT 2   Trials and Temptations

James 1:2-18

Trials and Temptations

²Consider it pure joy, my brothers, whenever you face trials of many kinds, ³because you know that the testing of your faith develops perseverance. ⁴Perseverance must finish its work so that you may be mature and complete, not lacking anything. ⁵If any of you lacks wisdom, he should ask God, who gives generously to all without finding fault, and it will be given to him. ⁶But when he asks, he must believe and not doubt, because he who doubts is like a wave of the sea, blown and tossed by the wind. ⁷That man should not think he will receive anything from the Lord; ⁸he is a double-minded man, unstable in all he does.

⁹The brother in humble circumstances ought to take pride in his high position. ¹⁰But the one who is rich should take pride in his low position, because he will pass away like a wild flower. ¹¹For the sun rises with scorching heat and withers the plant; its blossom falls and its beauty is destroyed. In the same way, the rich man will fade away even while he goes about his business.

¹²Blessed is the man who perseveres under trial, because when he has stood the test, he will receive the crown of life that God has promised to those who love him.

¹³When tempted, no one should say, "God is tempting me." For God cannot be tempted by evil, nor does he tempt anyone; ¹⁴but each one is tempted when, by his own evil desire, he is dragged away and enticed. ¹⁵Then, after desire has conceived, it gives birth to sin; and sin, when it is full-grown, gives birth to death.

¹⁶Don't be deceived, my dear brothers. ¹⁷Every good and perfect gift is from above, coming down from the Father of the heavenly lights, who does not change like shifting shadows. ¹⁸He chose to give us birth through the word of truth, that we might be a kind of firstfruits of all he created.

Questions

OPEN: 1. Would you describe yourself more as a gullible "Winnie-the-Pooh" type, or as a skeptical "Eeyore" type? Why? Give an example where you bought something fishy "hook, line, and sinker." **2.** As a child, what was one birthday or Christmas gift you especially remember receiving? What good gift do you prize from your purchases at garage sales?

DIG: 1. What three themes are introduced here? How are they related to each other? **2.** How does James view hardships (vv.2-4,12)? How does he view wisdom? Perseverance? How do you view them? **3.** What kind of "wisdom" was needed in those times? What are the conditions for receiving wisdom? Is doubt ever to be expressed? How so? **4.** Who are these "poor" and "rich" (vv.9-11; see notes)? What would a person in humble circumstances have to "take pride in"? What is "low" about a rich person's position? What is the practical difference between "trials" and "temptations"? How does the birth process illustrate verses 14-15? How is this related to gifts from God (vv.16-18)?

REFLECT: 1. Concerning a trial you have experienced, what pressures did it bring on your faith? What "wisdom" did you gain through it? **2.** Given the importance of wealth in modern society, what do verses 9-11 mean to you? What might James tell you to "take pride in"? **3.** What are the warning signs that you are being "enticed" by your evil desires? What helps you break the spell? **4.** What is a "good and perfect gift" for which you are thankful?

Notes

1:2 *consider it pure joy*. Christians ought to view the difficulties of life with enthusiasm, because the outcome of trials will be beneficial. The joy James is talking about is not just a feeling, however. It is an active acceptance of adversity. ***trials of many kinds***. The word "trials" has the dual sense of "adversity" (e.g., disease, persecution, tragedy) and "temptations" (e.g., lust, greed, trust in wealth).

1:3 One reason that the Christian can rejoice in suffering is because immediate good does come out of the pain. In this verse James *assumes* that there will be good results. ***perseverance***. Or "endurance." It is used in the sense of active overcoming, rather than passive acceptance.

1:4 *finish its work*. Perfection is not automatic—it takes time and effort. ***mature and complete***. What James has in mind here is wholeness of character. He is not calling for some sort of esoteric perfection or sinlessness. Instead, the emphasis is on moral blamelessness. He is thinking of the integrated life, in contrast to the divided person of verses 6-8.

1:5 *wisdom*. This is not just abstract knowledge, but God-given insight which leads to right living. It is the ability to make right decisions, especially about moral issues (as one must do during trials).

1:6 James now contrasts the readiness on God's part to give (v.5) with the hesitation on people's part to ask (v.6). Both here and in 4:3, unanswered prayer is connected to the quality of the asking, not to the unwillingness of God to give. ***believe***. To be in *one mind* about God's ability to answer prayer, to be sure that God will hear and will act in accord with his superior wisdom.

1:8 *double-minded*. To doubt is to be in *two minds*—to believe and to disbelieve simultaneously.

1:9-11 Poverty is an example of a trial to be endured—but so too are riches, though in quite a different way. The question of riches and poverty is the third major theme in the book.

1:9 *humble circumstances*. Those who are poor in a material and social sense, and who are looked down on by others because they are poor. ***take pride***. This becomes possible when the poor see beyond immediate circumstances to their new position as children of God. They may be poor in

worldly goods, but they are rich beyond imagining since they are children of God. ***high position***. In the early Church, the poor gained a new sense of self-respect. Slaves found that traditional social distinctions had been obliterated (Gal 3:28).

1:10 *rich*. The peril of riches is that people come to trust in wealth as a source of security. It is a mark of double-mindedness to attempt to serve both God and money. The word "rich," in James, "always indicates one outside the community, a non-believing person. The rich, in fact, are the oppressors of the community (2:6; 5:1-6)" (Davids). ***low position***. Jewish culture understood wealth to be a sure sign of God's favor. Here, as elsewhere (vv.2,9), James reverses conventional expectations.

1:12-27 James now launches into the second statement of his three themes. He will discuss trials (vv.12-18), speech (vv.19-21), and generosity (vv.22-27).

1:12 *blessed*. Happy is he or she who has withstood all the trials to the end. ***perseveres***. In verse 3, James says that testing produces perseverance. Here he points out that such perseverance brings the reward of blessedness. ***stood the test***. Such a person is like metal which has been purged by fire and is purified of all foreign substances. ***crown of life***. As with Paul (Ro 5:1-5) and Peter (1Pe 1:6-7), James now focuses on the final result of endurance under trial: eternal life.

1:13-15 Perseverance under trial is not the only option. People can fail. In these verses James examines the causes of such failure.

1:13 *tempted*. The focus shifts from *enduring* outward trials (v.12) to *resisting* inner temptations. ***"God is tempting me."*** The natural tendency is to blame others for our failure (in this case, God). But according to James, God does not put people into situations in order to test them. Such temptations arise quite naturally from life itself.

1:14-15 The steps in temptation are explained by reference to the birth process ("conceived," "birth," "full-grown"). The possibility of an evil act is entertained, then acted on again and again (the thought becomes deed) until it finally brings death.

1:16-18 Far from tempting people, God gives gifts, most notably the gift of new life.

UNIT 3   Listening and Doing

James 1:19-27

Listening and Doing

[19]My dear brothers, take note of this: Everyone should be quick to listen, slow to speak and slow to become angry, [20]for man's anger does not bring about the righteous life that God desires. [21]Therefore, get rid of all moral filth and the evil that is so prevalent and humbly accept the word planted in you, which can save you.

[22]Do not merely listen to the word, and so deceive yourselves. Do what it says. [23]Anyone who listens to the word but does not do what it says is like a man who looks at his face in a mirror [24]and, after looking at himself, goes away and immediately forgets what he looks like. [25]But the man who looks intently into the perfect law that gives freedom, and continues to do this, not forgetting what he has heard, but doing it—he will be blessed in what he does.

[26]If anyone considers himself religious and yet does not keep a tight rein on his tongue, he deceives himself and his religion is worthless. [27]Religion that God our Father accepts as pure and faultless is this: to look after orphans and widows in their distress and to keep oneself from being polluted by the world.

Questions

OPEN: 1. Which best describes your temper: Short fuse, big bomb? Long fuse, little fizz? Long fuse, H-bomb? Give an example. **2.** What things are you sure to check in a mirror for, prior to leaving the house in the morning?

DIG: 1. Illustrate "quick to listen." How does this produce the "righteous life that God desires" (v.19)? **2.** What is the point of the mirror imagery? How is this point reflected in worthless religion? In pure religion (vv.26-27)?

REFLECT: 1. Think of one significant relationship you have. What would have changed if you had applied verses 19-20 with that person this week? **2.** How would you characterize your religion: Worthless? Pure? Activist? Pious? Charitable? Self-fulfilling? Self-emptying? Think of an example from last week. **3.** What will you do this week to practice your religion?

Notes

1:19-21 Having just mentioned God's word (v.18), James shifts here to the subject of human words. From the "word of truth" he moves to the "word of anger." James is still, in fact, focusing on the theme of wisdom, except that now his concern is with the relationship between wisdom and speech—a connection he will make plainer in 3:1-4:12. James 1:16-18 parallels this section. There he pointed out that wisdom is a gift of God. Here he points out that the wise person is slow to speak.

1:19b The heart of what James wants to say is found in this proverb. **slow to speak**. One needs to consider carefully what is to be said, rather than impulsively and carelessly launching into words that are not wise. **slow to become angry**. James does not forbid anger. However, James does caution against responding in anger at every opportunity.

1:20 This verse is reminiscent of what Jesus said in the Sermon on the Mount (Mt 5:21-22). **the righteous life**. Human anger does not produce the kind of life that God wants.

1:21 If Christians are to speak wisely, they must prepare to do so by the dual action of ridding themselves of all that is corrupt (and not of God), and then by humbly relying upon the word of God which is within them already. **get rid of**. This verb means literally, "to lay aside" or "to strip off," as one would do with filthy clothing. To be in tune with God's purpose first requires this negative action—this rejection or repentance of all that drags one down. **all moral filth and the evil**. The two Greek words here refer to actual dirt and are used as a metaphor for moral uncleanness. Given the context, they probably refer primarily to vulgar and malicious speech (Laws). The second word has proven very difficult to translate properly. In the King James Bible it is translated "superfluity of naughtiness." The New English Bible renders it "reckless dissipation"; whereas Beza translates it simply as "excrement." **humbly accept**. Having renounced evil (a negative act), the next step is to accept that which is good (a positive act). This same two-fold action of repentance and faith (rejecting evil and accepting God) is the path whereby people come to Christian faith in the first place. Repentance and faith are also the key to living out the Christian life.

James has already twice mentioned the idea of receiving God's gifts (vv.5 and 17). This receiving must be done **humbly**. This attitude contrasts directly with anger about which he just spoke. **the word**. This is the same "word of truth" mentioned in verse 18. In contrast to the quick and angry words of people (words which hurt and destroy), there is the word of God which saves. **planted in you**. They are Christians already. They have the life of God in them. It is now up to them to act upon what is already theirs. They must actualize in their lives the truth of God.

1:22-27 The concept of *accepting* the word of God (v.21) leads James to the concept of *doing* the word of God. Thus he moves from proper speech to proper action, which in this case is charity toward those in need. In this way he gets to his third theme, the idea that Christians are called upon to be generous in the face of poverty.

1:22 merely listen. The Christian must not just hear the word of God. A response is required. **deceive yourself**. It does not matter how well a person may know the teaching of the apostles or how much Scripture he or she has memorized. To make mere knowledge of God's will the sole criterion for the religious life is dangerous and self-deceptive. **Do what it says**. This is James' main point in this section.

1:23-24 James illustrates his point with a metaphor. The person who reads Scripture (which is a mirror to the Christian, because in it his or her true state is shown) and then goes away unchanged is like the person who gets up in the morning and sees how dirty and disheveled he is, but then promptly forgets about it (when the proper response would be to get cleaned up).

1:25 In contrast is the person who not only acts to correct what is discovered to be wrong but then goes on acting in this way. **the perfect law**. The reference is probably to the teachings of Jesus which set one free, in contradistinction to the oral Jewish law which brought bondage (see Ro 8:2). **continues**. Such people do not happen to notice a command and then act on it once, they make that insight a *continuing* part of their lives. **blessed**. The sheer act of keeping the law is a happy experience in and of itself because it produces good fruit, now and in the future.

UNIT 4   Favoritism Forbidden

James 2:1-13

Questions

Favoritism Forbidden

2 My brothers, as believers in our glorious Lord Jesus Christ, don't show favoritism. [2]Suppose a man comes into your meeting wearing a gold ring and fine clothes, and a poor man in shabby clothes also comes in. [3]If you show special attention to the man wearing fine clothes and say, "Here's a good seat for you," but say to the poor man, "You stand there" or "Sit on the floor by my feet," [4]have you not discriminated among yourselves and become judges with evil thoughts?

[5]Listen, my dear brothers: Has not God chosen those who are poor in the eyes of the world to be rich in faith and to inherit the kingdom he promised those who love him? [6]But you have insulted the poor. Is it not the rich who are exploiting you? Are they not the ones who are dragging you into court? [7]Are they not the ones who are slandering the noble name of him to whom you belong?

[8]If you really keep the royal law found in Scripture, "Love your neighbor as yourself,"[a] you are doing right. [9]But if you show favoritism, you sin and are convicted by the law as lawbreakers. [10]For whoever keeps the whole law and yet stumbles at just one point is guilty of breaking all of it. [11]For he who said, "Do not commit adultery,"[b] also said, "Do not murder."[c] If you do not commit adultery but do commit murder, you have become a lawbreaker.

[12]Speak and act as those who are going to be judged by the law that gives freedom, [13]because judgment without mercy will be shown to anyone who has not been merciful. Mercy triumphs over judgment!

OPEN: 1. For what event would you buy the "best seats": The World Series? Carnegie Hall? Your child's school play? **2.** In your family tree, do you have anyone who lived in "dirt poor" conditions? Any in "filthy rich" conditions? Any go from "rags to riches"? Contrast any two branches of your family tree in terms of what they've got and what they lack.

DIG: 1. James is writing to an economically depressed community. Why would favoritism be a problem in this setting? **2.** For what reasons does James oppose favoritism (vv.4-13)? What kinds of distinctions between people are acceptable in God's eyes? If God sides with the poor (widows, orphans, etc.), is he playing favorites, or what? **3.** What is the "law" (vv.8-12; see 1:25)? Its purpose? Its consequences? In this context, how is "mercy" and "judgment" related to law?

REFLECT: 1. To you, who are people with "gold rings" today: The rich? Powerful? Athletic? "Mr. Right"? **2.** Who are "the poor": The uneducated? Those of another race? The divorced? What would change if you applied the "royal law" to them? If society as a whole did? **3.** How has favoritism in Christian circles affected you?

---

[a]*8* Lev. 19:18   [b]*11* Exodus 20:14; Deut. 5:18   [c]*11* Exodus 20:13; Deut. 5:17

Notes

2:1-13 James now begins his exposition of his first theme: poverty and generosity (2:1-26). Notice that he treats these themes in the reverse order from which he presented them in his introduction. In this chapter his focus is on the question of the rich and the poor. Christians are to have a different ethic than that of the world. They are not to favor the wealthy simply because they are wealthy, nor are they to despise the poor simply because they are poor. The poor are to be welcomed and aided. In fact, one's faith is shown by acts of generosity to the poor. The first half of the chapter (2:1-13) focuses on a warning against prejudice.

2:1-9 James' point is quite straightforward: to discriminate between people is inconsistent with the Christian faith.

2:1 *glorious*. Jesus is described here by means of a word that denotes the presence of God. When God draws near, what people experience is the light of his splendor. James' point is that in Jesus one sees a manifestation of God's presence. *favoritism*. This is the act of paying special attention to someone because he or she is rich, important, famous, powerful, etc.

2:2-4 James now gives a specific example of how deference to the rich operates in the church. The situation he describes could well have happened in the first-century church. It was one of the few institutions where traditional social barriers had been dropped. It would have been quite possible for a wealthy landowner to belong to the same Christian assembly as one of his slaves.

2:2 *a gold ring*. This is the mark of those who belonged to the equestrian order—the second level of Roman aristocracy. These noblemen were typically wealthy. Rings (in general) were a sign of wealth. The more ostentatious would fill their fingers with rings. Early Christians were urged to wear only one ring, on the little finger, bearing the image of a dove, fish, or anchor. *poor man*. The word used here denotes a beggar, a person from the lowest level of society. Had this been a low-paid worker, a different Greek word would have been used.

2:4-7 James attacks this kind of discrimination. All social distinctions are null and void in the church.

Partiality is clearly out of place. Both rich and poor are to be received equally. Notice that the rich are not condemned here, *per se*. They are welcome in the church. What is condemned is the insult to the poor person (v.6).

2:5 *those who are poor*. The New Testament is clearly on the side of the poor. In Jesus' first sermon he declared that he was called to preach the gospel to the poor (Lk 4:18). When John the Baptist questioned whether Jesus was actually the Messiah, in response Jesus pointed to his preaching to the poor (Mt 11:4-5). The poor are called blessed (Lk 6:20). The poor flocked to Jesus during his ministry and later into his Church (1Co 1:26). As William Barclay wrote: "It is not that Christ and the Church do not want the great and the rich and the wise and the mighty...but it was the simple fact that the gospel offered so much to the poor and demanded so much from the rich, that it was the poor who were swept into the Church."

2:6 *exploiting you*. In a day of abject poverty the poor were often forced to borrow money at exorbitant rates of interest just to survive. The rich profited from their need. *dragging you into court*. This was probably over the issue of a debt. "If a creditor met a debtor on the streets, he could seize him by the neck of his robe, nearly throttling him and literally drag him to the law courts" (Barclay).

2:7 Not only do they exploit the poor and harass them in court, they also mock the name of Jesus. *the royal law*. The law of love is the central moral principle by which Christians are to order their lives (see Mk 12:28-33).

2:10-13 Favoritism is not just transgression of a single law. In fact, it makes one answerable to the whole law. The Jews thought of law-keeping in terms of credit and debit: did your good deeds outweigh The idea of *judgment* is connected to the need for *mercy*. In fact, what James is calling for in verses 2-3 is *mercy* for the poor. Christians are not bound by rigid laws by which they will one day be judged, as Judaism taught. So the fear of future punishment is not a deterrent to behavior. Rather, it is the inner compulsion of love that motivates the Christian to right action.

UNIT 5   Faith and Deeds

James 2:14-26

Faith and Deeds

[14]What good is it, my brothers, if a man claims to have faith but has no deeds? Can such faith save him? [15]Suppose a brother or sister is without clothes and daily food. [16]If one of you says to him, "Go, I wish you well; keep warm and well fed," but does nothing about his physical needs, what good is it? [17]In the same way, faith by itself, if it is not accompanied by action, is dead.

[18]But someone will say, "You have faith; I have deeds."

Show me your faith without deeds, and I will show you my faith by what I do. [19]You believe that there is one God. Good! Even the demons believe that—and shudder.

[20]You foolish man, do you want evidence that faith without deeds is useless[d]? [21]Was not our ancestor Abraham considered righteous for what he did when he offered his son Isaac on the altar? [22]You see that his faith and his actions were working together, and his faith was made complete by what he did. [23]And the scripture was fulfilled that says, "Abraham believed God, and it was credited to him as righteousness,"[e] and he was called God's friend. [24]You see that a person is justified by what he does and not by faith alone.

[25]In the same way, was not even Rahab the prostitute considered righteous for what she did when she gave lodging to the spies and sent them off in a different direction? [26]As the body without the spirit is dead, so faith without deeds is dead.

Questions

OPEN: Are you a doer or a thinker? Are you more likely to act without thinking, or think without acting? Give an example.

DIG: 1. Pretend the scene in verses 15-17 happened in your church this Sunday. Role play how "faith *without* works" differs from "faith *with* works." What is the underlying problem here? The solution? **2.** How do Abraham (Ge 22) and Rahab (Jos 2) prove James' point (see notes)? **3.** How is Paul's argument in Romans 3:28 different from James' point in 2:24 (see notes)? **4.** What kind of faith is James or Paul criticizing, and why: Intellectual faith? Invisible faith? Inconsistent faith? Orthodox faith? Incomplete faith? Ignorant faith? Inward faith? Saving faith? Sanctifying faith? Works-oriented faith? Ritual-keeping? **5.** Of these, which kind are they each commending, and why?

REFLECT: If you were arrested for being a Christian, what evidence would be used to prove the point? From 1:22-27 and 2:14-17, what further evidence do you want to provide this week?

---

[d]20 Some early manuscripts *dead*   [e]23 Gen. 15:6

46

Notes

2:14-26 This is part two of James' discussion of the poor. In part one (2:1-13) the issue was discrimination against the poor. Here the issue is charity toward the poor.

2:14 *faith*. James uses this word in a special way. The faith he speaks of here is mere intellectual affirmation. Such a mind-oriented profession stands in sharp contrast to the comprehensive, whole-life commitment that characterizes true New Testament faith. New Testament faith involves believing with all one's being: mind, emotions, body (behavior), and spirit. The people James has in mind differ from their pagan and Jewish neighbors only in what they profess to believe. They are orthodox Christians who believe in Jesus; however, they live no differently than anyone else. *deeds*. Just as James uses the word "faith" in his own way, so too his use of *deeds* (or "works"). For James, deeds have to do with proper ethical behavior. **Can such faith save him?** The implied answer to this rhetorical question is "No." This answer is based on what James just said in 2:12-13. Intellectual faith cannot save one from judgment when one has not been merciful.

2:15 *Suppose*. A test case is proposed through which the absurdity of claiming "faith" without corresponding "action" is made evident.

2:16 The implication is that the Christian to whom this appeal has been made could meet the need but choses not to and instead offers pious platitudes.

2:17 James did not dream up his conclusion here. It is what is taught consistently throughout the New Testament. John the Baptist taught it (Lk 3:8). Jesus taught it (Mt 5:16; 7:15-21). And Paul taught it (Ro 2:6; 14:12; 1Co 3:8; 2Co 5:10). *dead*. James is saying: "Your faith is not real, it is a sham. You are playing at being a Christian."

2:18 *But someone will say*. James responds to an imaginary critic who raises a new issue. This person contends that both faith and deeds are good on their own. "Some have faith. Others perform deeds. Both are praiseworthy. In either case, a person is religious." James disagrees that faith and deeds are unconnected.

It is not a matter of either/or. It is both/and (as he shows in v.22). **Show me your faith without deeds**. James replies that faith is invisible without deeds. If faith does not make itself known in one's lifestyle, then it is non-existent. Deeds are the only demonstration of inner faith.

2:20 *You foolish man*. The NIV blunts the harshness of James' language here. "You fool," he is saying. "You empty man," which is the literal rendering of this phrase.

2:21-25 James concludes by offering via two illustrations from the Old Testament the evidence demanded by the fool in verse 20 for the assertion that faith is useless without deeds. In both cases faith is demonstrated by means of concrete action. Abraham actually had the knife raised over his beloved son Issac, and Rahab actually hid the spies. Without faith, Abraham would never have even considered sacrificing his only son, nor would Rahab have defied her king at great personal risk.

2:22 The heart of James' argument: faith and deeds working together characterize the life of the person who is truly religious. *actions*. This is plural because Abraham's action with Isaac was not an isolated instance, but the culmination of many actions based on faith in God. *made complete*. The idea is not that faith is somehow perfected by deeds. Rather, faith is brought to new maturity by such actions.

2:23-24 Paul uses this same verse (Ge 15:6) to demonstrate the *opposite* point in Romans 4, namely that it was not by his deed but by his faith that Abraham was justified. But, in fact, Paul and James use this verse in quite different ways. Paul's point is that Abraham believed God and was declared righteous *prior to* the ritual action (the deed) of circumcision. But James focuses on the offering up of Isaac (Ge 22:2, 9-10)—not on the act of circumcision—and declares that this act of offering up his son demonstrated that Abraham had faith. Furthermore, the works Paul has in mind are acts of ritual law-keeping such as circumcision, food laws, and the like; whereas for James it is acts of charity that he is concerned about, not fulfillment of the law.

UNIT 6   Taming the Tongue

James 3:1-12

Taming the Tongue

3 Not many of you should presume to be teachers, my brothers, because you know that we who teach will be judged more strictly. ²We all stumble in many ways. If anyone is never at fault in what he says, he is a perfect man, able to keep his whole body in check.

³When we put bits into the mouths of horses to make them obey us, we can turn the whole animal. ⁴Or take ships as an example. Although they are so large and are driven by strong winds, they are steered by a very small rudder wherever the pilot wants to go. ⁵Likewise the tongue is a small part of the body, but it makes great boasts. Consider what a great forest is set on fire by a small spark. ⁶The tongue also is a fire, a world of evil among the parts of the body. It corrupts the whole person, sets the whole course of his life on fire, and is itself set on fire by hell.

⁷All kinds of animals, birds, reptiles and creatures of the sea are being tamed and have been tamed by man, ⁸but no man can tame the tongue. It is a restless evil, full of deadly poison.

⁹With the tongue we praise our Lord and Father, and with it we curse men, who have been made in God's likeness. ¹⁰Out of the same mouth come praise and cursing. My brothers, this should not be. ¹¹Can both fresh water and salt^f water flow from the same spring? ¹²My brothers, can a fig tree bear olives, or a grapevine bear figs? Neither can a salt spring produce fresh water.

Questions

OPEN: What symptoms of "foot-in-mouth disease" have you recently demonstrated? What is one of your best-known "bloopers"?

DIG: 1. Why is a stricter judgment placed upon teachers? How does this warning relate to taming the tongue? **2.** Which of these common criticisms of teachers would James agree with, and why: (a) Biased (toward the rich, who favor them)? (b) Hypocritical (say one thing and do another)? (c) Too educated for their own (or others') good? (d) Irrelevant (or stuck in an ivory tower)? (e) Responsible for their captive congregations? (f) Too glib with the tongue? **3.** What do the three illustrations here (horse's bit, ship's rudder, fire's spark) each reveal about the tongue's power? **4.** From the next set of illustrations (vv.11-12; see notes), how can people *both* curse others *and* praise God? What does this say about the tongue? About human nature? About hope for change?

REFLECT: When do you feel like your tongue is "set on fire by hell"? What have you found to be helpful in controlling your tongue? In changing the source of its spring (v.11)?

---

^{f}11 Greek *bitter* (see also verse 14)

Notes

3:1-12 James now shifts to his second subject: wisdom. This discussion will extend from 3:1 to 4:12. In this first section, he examines the connection between speech and wisdom. In particular, he focuses on the tongue, that organ by which we produce words, the vehicles of wisdom. Words, he says, are not insignificant. Words can be wise but they can also be deadly. The tongue is such a small organ, yet it has great power. It can control the very direction of one's life. Mature people are known by their ability to control the tongue.

3:1 Not many of you should presume to become teachers. In the early church a person did not become a teacher by going to seminary or Bible school. None existed. Instead, teachers were called and empowered by the Holy Spirit (see Ro 12:6-7; 1Co 12:28; and Eph 4:11-13). The problem was that the gift of teaching could be imitated. It was a prestigious position and if a person were eloquent, he or she might pretend to be a teacher. False teachers were a real problem in the first century (see 1Ti 1:7; Tit 1:11; and 2Pe 2:1.) **judged more strictly**. It is dangerous to feign the gift of teaching (see Mt 12:36; 23:1-33; and Mk 12:40.) To mislead God's people by false words or an inappropriate lifestyle can cause great harm to those seeking to know God and follow his ways.

3:2 stumble. This word means "to trip, to slip up, or to make a mistake." This is not deliberate, premeditated wrongdoing. Rather, it is failure due to inadequacy. This is a problem of faulty *reactions*, not evil *actions*. **what he says**. James' focus is on words, the stock-in-trade of teachers. Thus James launches into the main theme of this section: the sins of the tongue. It is important to notice that James is not calling here for silence, only for control (see 1:19). **perfect**. This same word is also used in 1:4 and in 1:25. In all three instances, it is used to describe that which is mature, complete, and whole. James is not teaching that Christians should be morally perfect, living in a state of sinlessness.

3:3-4 horses. These huge, powerful animals can be controlled and guided by the human rider simply by means of a small bit. **ships**. Ships were among the largest man-made objects that first-century people would have seen. That such a big structure driven by such powerful forces ("strong winds") could be controlled by so small a device as a rudder amply illustrates what James wants to say about the tongue. The person who controls the bit or rudder (or tongue) has control over the horse or ship (or the body).

3:6 This is a notoriously difficult verse to translate and to understand. The general sense, however, is clear. The tongue is like a fire. It is capable of corrupting the whole person. Speech can burst forth into evil action.

3:7 tame. The Old Testament states that one of the functions of human beings is to domesticate the animal kingdom (see Ge 1:28; 9:2; Ps 8:6-8). Yet despite our ability to control all four classes of animals (mammals, bird, amphibians, and fish), we remain unable to subdue our own tongues. **reptiles**. In the Greco-Roman world, serpents were thought to have healing power, and so the ill slept among tame snakes in the temples of Aesculapius. The modern symbol used by the medical profession has a snake entwined around a shaft.

3:8 restless. The same word is used in 1:8 and is translated there as "unstable." There it is used to describe the double-minded person. In 3:9 the dual nature of the tongue will be emphasized. **deadly poison**. As with serpents, so human tongues can bring death as well (see Ps 58:3-5; 140:3).

3:9 with the tongue we praise. The tongue is vital to all worship: praying, singing, praising, and thanking. Devout Jews offered praise to God three times a day. **we**. Everybody, even James, has the same problem with the tongue. **curse men**. It is by means of words that people bring real harm to others. **in God's likeness**. Since people are made in the image of God, when they are cursed, God too is being cursed. The same tongue that praises God is also used to curse him, a point James makes explicit in verse 10.

3:11-12 James ends with three illustrations from nature which show how unnatural it is for human beings to use the same vehicle to utter praises and curses. Nothing in nature is like that, he says. A spring gives one type of water only: fresh water or brackish water. A tree bears only a single species of fruit.

UNIT 7   Two Kinds of Wisdom

James 3:13-18

Two Kinds of Wisdom

[13]Who is wise and understanding among you? Let him show it by his good life, by deeds done in the humility that comes from wisdom. [14]But if you harbor bitter envy and selfish ambition in your hearts, do not boast about it or deny the truth. [15]Such "wisdom" does not come down from heaven but is earthly, unspiritual, of the devil. [16]For where you have envy and selfish ambition, there you find disorder and every evil practice.

[17]But the wisdom that comes from heaven is first of all pure; then peace-loving, considerate, submissive, full of mercy and good fruit, impartial and sincere. [18]Peacemakers who sow in peace raise a harvest of righteousness.

Questions

OPEN: 1. What describes you best when working with a committee: A busy bee? A hibernating bear? A wise old owl? A prowling lion? **2.** As such, are you more likely to "say what you mean" (emphasis on correct speech), or "mean what you say" (emphasis on follow-up action)?

DIG: 1. How do these two kinds of wisdom differ as to their source? Their symptoms? Their results? **2.** What is the model here for effective managers, teachers, pastors, and parents?

REFLECT: 1. How is "earthly wisdom" hurting you? **2.** In which area do you need heaven's wisdom? How will you cultivate that?

Notes

3:13-18 This is part two of James' discussion of wisdom. In it, he probes why on the one hand, speech can be so destructive yet on the other hand, there are teachers in the church (of which he is one) who communicate true wisdom. His conclusion is that it all depends on the *source* of the words. In this unit, he distinguishes between wisdom from above and wisdom from below. This unit not only looks backward to the problem of destructive speech (3:1-12), but it also looks forward to the problem such uncontrolled speech has brought to the Christian community—the issue James will deal with in next section (4:1-12).

3:13 Who is wise...among you? James is probably thinking of the problem of false teachers which he raised in 3:1. Yet given the fact that wisdom is a major theme of this book as he indicated in his introduction (see 1:5-8,16-21), these words are also intended for all Christians to hear and heed. **Let him show it**. The same problem faces the Christian who claims to have "faith" as faces the one who claims to have "understanding." Both of these qualities are interior. Neither can be seen directly. Both must be demonstrated. As James argued in chapter two, faith is shown via the deeds it inspires. But how is understanding shown? **by his good life, by deeds**. It might be anticipated that understanding would be demonstrated by means of speech. Those who had the most understanding would possess the best verbal skills. They would be the popular teachers or the clever debaters. But this is not what James says. Understanding, like faith, is shown by *how one lives*. Specifically, understanding is demonstrated by a good life and by good deeds. Those who truly "understand" will live the kind of life that displays such understanding. This is also what Jesus taught (see Mt 7:15-23.)

3:14-16 Having described how true wisdom shows itself, James now turns to a description of how "pretend" wisdom displays itself. "James is concerned to show his readers that any claim to wisdom is vitiated by such behavior as he describes: it becomes a 'non-wisdom.' His point is not that there is a different wisdom in opposition to the true one, but that a claim to true wisdom

cannot be upheld in the context of an inconsistent style of life" (Laws).

3:14 Envy and ambition are the marks of false teachers. James is probably referring to the teachers he mentioned in 3:1 who are rivals vying for positions of authority within the Jerusalem church. Such competition clearly violates the nature of wisdom. **bitter envy**. The word translated "bitter" is the same word which was used in verse 12 to describe brackish water unfit for human consumption. It is now applied to zeal (the word translated "envy" is literally *zelos*). Zeal that has gone astray becomes jealousy. **selfish ambition**. The word translated here as "selfish ambition" originally meant "those who can be hired to do spinning." Then it came to mean "those who work for pay." It later came to mean "those who work only for what they get out of it" and it was applied to those who sought political office merely for personal gain (Barclay). **in your hearts**. This is the issue. What lies at the core of the person's being? Is it true wisdom from God or is it ambition? True wisdom will show itself via a good life filled with loving deeds done in a humble spirit. But envy and ambition will display itself by quite a different sort of life (which James will describe more fully in v.16). **do not boast about it or deny the truth**. Those whose hearts are filled with this sense of rivalry and party spirit ought not to pretend that they are speaking God's wisdom. That is merely to compound the wrong.

3:15 James uses three terms—each of which is less desirable than the previous one—to describe the true origin of this "non-wisdom." There is "earthly" wisdom which arises out of this world. There is "unspiritual" wisdom which arises out of the "soul" of the person. Neither form of wisdom is necessarily bad, except when it claims to originate with the Spirit of God. And then there is wisdom "of the devil" which is not neutral. This is lit., "demon-like"; i.e., that which is possessed even by demons (see 2:19) or which is under the control of evil spirits.

3:16-18 James contrasts the lifestyle that emerges from pretend wisdom (v.16) with that which arises out of true wisdom (vv.17-18).

UNIT 8   Submit Yourselves to God

James 4:1-12

Submit Yourselves to God

4 What causes fights and quarrels among you? Don't they come from your desires that battle within you? ²You want something but don't get it. You kill and covet, but you cannot have what you want. You quarrel and fight. You do not have, because you do not ask God. ³When you ask, you do not receive, because you ask with wrong motives, that you may spend what you get on your pleasures.

⁴You adulterous people, don't you know that friendship with the world is hatred toward God? Anyone who chooses to be a friend of the world becomes an enemy of God. ⁵Or do you think Scripture says without reason that the spirit he caused to live in us envies intensely?ᵍ ⁶But he gives us more grace. That is why Scripture says:

> "God opposes the proud
>   but gives grace to the humble."ʰ

⁷Submit yourselves, then, to God. Resist the devil, and he will flee from you. ⁸Come near to God and he will come near to you. Wash your hands, you sinners, and purify your hearts, you double-minded. ⁹Grieve, mourn and wail. Change your laughter to mourning and your joy to gloom. ¹⁰Humble yourselves before the Lord, and he will lift you up.

¹¹Brothers, do not slander one another. Anyone who speaks against his brother or judges him speaks against the law and judges it. When you judge the law, you are not keeping it, but sitting in judgment on it. ¹²There is only one Lawgiver and Judge, the one who is able to save and destroy. But you—who are you to judge your neighbor?

Questions

OPEN: 1. Over what (and with whom) did you quarrel most when you were a kid? **2.** What purchase is highest on your "wish list" now? Why?

DIG: 1. From what does this strife (vv.1,11) come: Persecution? Possessiveness? Private pleasures? Misguided prayer? Frustrated desire (see 1:14)? **2.** How is James' ten-fold prescription (vv.7-10) an effective antidote? Why the switch to the imperative voice ("Do this, do that")? How is this cure related to other themes in James? **3.** What is meant by "adulterous people" (v.4), "friendship with the world" (v.4), and submission to God (vv.7-10)? Give examples. **4.** What are some outward signs of this inner submission to God? **5.** Is the "law" in verse 11 the same as that in 1:25? 2:8? 2:12? Why or why not? How does grace (v.6) relate to this law?

REFLECT: 1. What is your usual response when your desires are frustrated? Where does that get you? **2.** How is the "world" trying to get you to be its "friend" now? How is that related to your faithfulness to God? **3.** How is James' cure (vv. 7-10) applicable to you as you struggle with the world's seduction?

ᵍ5   Or *that God jealously longs for the spirit that he made to live in us*; or *that the Spirit he caused to live in us longs jealously*   ʰ6   Prov. 3:34

Notes

4:1-12 The final part of James' discussion about wisdom has to do with their life together as a church. Their failure to live out God's wisdom has had the most serious consequences. In the previous section (3:13-18), he mentioned in a general way the disorder and evil that came from envy and ambition. Now he gets quite specific.

4:1-3 James begins by naming the root cause of all this strife. It is the desire for pleasure.

4:1 *What causes fights and quarrels among you?* Where does all this strife come from? It is not initiated by the wise leaders who are peacemakers (3:18). It is not caused by persecution from the world. James is very clear that the strife is internal ("among you"). ***fights and quarrels***. Literally "wars and battles." These are long-term conflicts, not sudden explosions. ***desires***. Literally "pleasures." In Greek the word is *hedone*, from which our word "hedonism" is derived. James is not saying that personal pleasure is inherently wrong. However, there is a certain desire for gratification that springs from the wrong source and possesses a person in the pursuit of its fulfillment. ***within you***. The struggle is within a person—between the part of him or her which is controlled by the Holy Spirit and that which is controlled by the world.

4:2 *You want something*. This is desire at work (see 1:14). ***but don't get it***. This is desire frustrated. ***kill and covet***. This is how frustrated desire responds. It lashes out at others in anger and abuse. (This is "killing" in a metaphorical sense—see Mt 5:21-22.) It responds in jealousy to those who have what it wants. ***quarrel and fight***. But still they do not have what they desire so the hostile action continues. This mad desire-driven quest causes a person to disregard other people, trampling over them if necessary to get what they want. ***you do not ask God***. One reason for this frustrated desire is a lack of prayer.

4:3 James senses a protest: "But I did ask God and I didn't get it." So he qualifies the absolute assertion in verse 2. The desire expressed in prayer may be inappropriate. God will not grant this type of request. Christians pray "in the name of Jesus," implying submission to the will of God. They can ask for wisdom and always expect to get it (if they do not waver), as James explains in 1:5. But this is different than asking for something

to sate an illicit pleasure and expecting to get it. Prayer is not magic. "The implication is not that God will not give us things that give us pleasure. God is the gracious God who gives not only bread and water but also steak and wine (Phil. 4:12; Jesus was not known for fasting!). The point is that they are motivated by selfish desires and ask simply to gratify themselves. This is not the trusting child asking for a meal but the greedy child asking for the best piece or the spoiled child demanding his or her way. They are asking God to bless their schemes; God will have no part of it" (Davids, GNC).

4:6 But their case is not hopeless. God does give grace. Repentance is possible. They can turn from their misbehavior. ***grace***. To receive grace, a person must *ask* for it. To be able to ask, one must see the need to do so. The proud person can't and doesn't see such a need. Only the humble do.

4:7-10 By means of a series of ten commands, James tells them how to repent. He has switched to the imperative voice: "Do this," he says, "and you will escape the mess you have got yourselves in." Thus he tells them to submit, resist, come near, wash, purify, grieve, mourn, wail, change, and humble themselves. ***Submit yourselves then, to God***. His first and primary command. ***Resist the devil***. Submission to God begins with resistance to Satan. ***he will flee from you***. Since Satan has no ultimate power over a Christian, when resisted he withdraws. ***Wash your hands***. Originally this was a ritual requirement whereby one became ceremoniously clean in preparation for the worship of God (see Ex 30:19-21). Now it is a symbol of the sort of inner purity God desires. ***sinners***. Those whose lives have become more characteristic of the enemy than of God—lapsed or "worldly" Christians. ***mourn and wail***. When people realize that they have been leading self-centered lives, in disobedience to God and harmful to others, they often feel overwhelming grief.

4:11-12 James ends his section on wisdom and speech by moving from a general call to repentance (vv.7-10) to a specific form of wrongdoing that they must deal with. His focus is on the sin of judgment and the pride that underlies it. ***slander***. This is to speak evil about other people in their absence so that they are unable to defend themselves. The word means both *false* accusation and harsh (though perhaps accurate) *criticism*.

UNIT 9   Boasting About Tomorrow

James 4:13-17

Boasting About Tomorrow

¹³Now listen, you who say, "Today or tomorrow we will go to this or that city, spend a year there, carry on business and make money." ¹⁴Why, you do not even know what will happen tomorrow. What is your life? You are a mist that appears for a little while and then vanishes. ¹⁵Instead, you ought to say, "If it is the Lord's will, we will live and do this or that." ¹⁶As it is, you boast and brag. All such boasting is evil. ¹⁷Anyone, then, who knows the good he ought to do and doesn't do it, sins.

Questions

OPEN: 1. Are you a long-range planner, or do you take one day at a time? Illustrate. **2.** If you won the lottery, how would you use your first $100,000?

DIG: 1. Regarding *tomorrow,* what's wrong with the type of planning here (see notes)? What's wrong with "boasting"? With profit-making? **2.** What might be going on behind the scenes with these wealthy people (see notes)? Who are they? How are they violating the "royal law" (2:8)? **3.** What will happen to their wealth? What is the lesson in that?

REFLECT: 1. How does this passage relate to your plans for the future? How do you exclude God in your planning? How do you specifically involve him? **2.** What does James imply about a Christian's use of wealth and power?

Notes

4:13-17 James begins discussion of his third and final theme: testing. He will deal with this theme, at first, as it touches the issue of wealth. The problem is the difficulty that comes with being wealthy and the tensions this brings both on a personal level and for the whole community. In this first part of his discussion (4:13-17), he looks at the situation of a group of Christian businessmen—in particular at their "sins of omission."

4:13 Boasting about what will happen tomorrow is another example of human arrogance. It is in the same category as judging one another (vv.11-12). Judgment is arrogant because God is the only legitimate judge. Boasting about the future is arrogant because God is the only one who knows what will happen in the future. **Now listen**. This is literally "Come now." It stands in sharp contrast to the way James has been addressing his readers. In the previous section he called them "my brothers" (3:1,11). James reverts to this more impersonal language in addressing these merchants. **"Today or tomorrow we will go..."**. James lets us listen in on the plans of a group of businessmen. Possibly they are looking at a map together. In any case, they are planning for the future and are concerned with where they will go, how long they will stay, what they will do, and how much profit they will make. But "there is absolutely nothing about their desires for the future, their use of money, or their way of doing business that is any different from the rest of the world. Their worship may be exemplary, their personal morality, impeccable; but when it come to business they think entirely on a worldly plane" (Davids, GNC). **carry on business**. The word James use here is derived from the Greek word *emporos*, from which the English word "emporium" comes. It denotes wholesale merchants who traveled from city to city, buying and selling. A different word was used to describe local peddlers who had small businesses in the bazaars. The growth of cities and the increase of trade between them during the Græco-Roman era created great opportunities for making money.

4:14 *tomorrow*. All such planning presupposes that tomorrow will unfold like any other day, when in fact, the future is anything but secure (see Pr 27:1). **What is your life?** Is it not death that is the great unknown? Who can know when death will come and interrupt plans? "Their projections are made; their plans are laid. But it all hinges on a will higher than theirs, a God unconsulted in their planning. That very night disease might strike; suddenly their plans evaporate, their only trip being one on a bier to a cold grave. They are like the rich fool of Jesus' parable, who had made a large honest profit through the chance occurrences of farming. Feeling secure, he makes rational plans for a comfortable retirement. 'But God said to him, "You fool! This very night you will have to give up your life" ' (Lk 12:16-21). By thinking on the worldly plane, James' Christian business people have gained a false sense of security. They need to look death in the face and realize their lack of control over life" (Davids, GNC). *mist*. Hosea 13:3 says: "Therefore they will be like the morning mist, like the early dew that disappears, like chaff swirling from a threshing floor, like smoke escaping through a window."

4:17 Some feel that this proverb-like statement may, in fact, be a saying of Jesus that did not get recorded in the Gospel accounts. In any case, by it James points out the nature of so-called "sins of omission." In other words, it is sin when we fail to do what we ought to do. The more familiar definition is of "sins of commission" or wrongdoing (see 1Jn 3:4). In other words, sinning can be both active and passive. Christians can sin by doing what they ought not to do (law breaking); or by not doing what they know they should do (failure). **who knows the good**. James applies this principle to the merchants. It is not that they are cheating and stealing in the course of their business (that would be active wrongdoing). The problem is in what they fail to do. Generally James defines "the good" as acts of charity toward those in need. And certainly in the context of this letter, it would appear that these men are failing in their duty to the poor.

UNIT 10   Warning to Rich Oppressors

James 5:1-6

Warning to Rich Oppressors

5 Now listen, you rich people, weep and wail because of the misery that is coming upon you. ²Your wealth has rotted, and moths have eaten your clothes. ³Your gold and silver are corroded. Their corrosion will testify against you and eat your flesh like fire. You have hoarded wealth in the last days. ⁴Look! The wages you failed to pay the workmen who mowed your fields are crying out against you. The cries of the harvesters have reached the ears of the Lord Almighty. ⁵You have lived on earth in luxury and self-indulgence. You have fattened yourselves in the day of slaughter.' ⁶You have condemned and murdered innocent men, who were not opposing you.

Questions

OPEN: What experience most affected your social conscience?

DIG: 1. What is James saying about wealth: Is it sinful? Is it illusory? Hazardous to your health? A burdensome responsibility? A way to heaven? To hell? **2.** Who is James addressing as "rich people": Chrisian businessmen (as in 4:13-17)? Secular landowners? Today"s multi-national corporations?

REFLECT: What abuses by the rich occur in the late 20th century? How could your church, or even your small group, use its resources to help overcome such inequity?

'5 Or *yourselves as in a day of feasting*

Notes

5:1-6 James is still on the theme of wealth, but now he shows that riches are, indeed, a great burden when seen in eternal terms. In an unusually vivid passage, James points out the ultimate worthlessness of wealth in the face of the coming Judgment. Although he is addressing the rich directly, he is also warning Christians not to covet wealth. Wealth is an illusion. It gives one a false sense of security. Not only that, it is gained at the expense of the poor, even to the extent of depriving them of their lives. And all this so that the rich can live in self-indulgent ways. In the previous passage James was concerned with the merchant class; business people who were, in this case, Christians (4:13-17). In this passage, his focus is on the landowner class who were, by and large, non-Christians.

5:1 _rich people_. In the first century there was a great gulf between rich and poor. Whereas a poor laborer (as in v.4) might have received one denarius a day as wages, a rich widow was said to have cursed the scribes because they allowed her only 400 gold denari a day to spend on luxuries! **_weep_**. James says that the appropriate response for these wealthy non-Christians is tears. Their luxury is only for the moment. In contrast, in 1:2 and 12, he urged the poor Christians to rejoice because their present suffering will pass, bringing with it great reward. **_wail_**. This is a strong word meaning "to shriek" or "howl," and is used to describe the terror that will be felt by the damned. **_the misery that is coming_**. James is referring to the future Day of Judgment, an event that will take place when the Lord returns. The noun _misery_ is related (in the Greek) to the verb _grieve_ used in 4:9. However, there is an important difference between the two uses. In 4:9 the grieving was self-imposed, the result of seeing one's failure, and it had a good result. Repentance opened up one to grace. But here this wretchedness results from the horror of being judged.

5:2-3 James points to the three major forms of wealth in the first century (food, clothes, and precious metals) and describes the decay of each. Agricultural products like corn and oil will rot. Clothes will become moth-eaten. And even precious metal will corrode.

5:2 _clothes_. Garments were one of the main forms of wealth in the first century. They were used as a means of payment, given as gifts, and passed on to one's children. (See Ge 45:22; Jos 7:21; Jdg 14:12; 2Ki 5:5; and Ac 20:33.)

5:3 _corroded_. Gold and silver do not, of course, rust or corrode (though silver will tarnish). James is using hyperbole to make his point: no form of wealth will make a person immune from the final judgment. **_testify against you_**. The existence of rotten food, moth-eaten garments, and rusty coins will stand as a condemnation against the person. Instead of being stored, these goods should have been used to feed and clothe the poor. **_eat your flesh like fire_**. In a striking image, James pictures wealth as having now turned against the person and become part of the torment he or she must endure. Just as rust eats through metal, so too it will eat through the flesh of the rich (see Lk 16:19-31 and Mk 9:43). **_the last days_**. The early Christians felt that Jesus would return very shortly, to draw his people to himself and to establish his kingdom on earth. James' point is: how inappropriate it is to give your energies over to accumulating treasures when, in effect, time itself is drawing to a close. This is an example of the kind of arrogance and pride that plans boldly for the future as if a person could control what lies ahead (see 4:14-16).

5:4-6 James now gets very specific as he details how it is that these folks were able to accumulate such wealth. In particular he points to the injustices leveled against those who worked on the farms.

5:4 _wages you failed to pay_. If a laborer was not given his wages at the end of the day, his family would go hungry the next day. The Old Testament insists that it is wrong to withhold wages. A worker was to be paid immediately. **_the workman_**. In Palestine, day laborers were used to plant and harvest the crops. They were cheaper than slaves, since if a slave converted to Judaism, he or she had to be freed in the sabbatical year. **_fields_**. The Greek word means "estates." These were the large tracts of land owned by the very wealthy. **_crying out_**. This is a word used to describe the wild, incoherent cry of an animal.

5:6 There is yet another accusation against the rich: they use their wealth and power to oppress the poor, even to the point of death.

UNIT 11   Patience in Suffering

James 5:7-12

Patience in Suffering

⁷Be patient, then, brothers, until the Lord's coming. See how the farmer waits for the land to yield its valuable crop and how patient he is for the autumn and spring rains. ⁸You too, be patient and stand firm, because the Lord's coming is near. ⁹Don't grumble against each other, brothers, or you will be judged. The Judge is standing at the door!

¹⁰Brothers, as an example of patience in the face of suffering, take the prophets who spoke in the name of the Lord. ¹¹As you know, we consider blessed those who have persevered. You have heard of Job's perseverance and have seen what the Lord finally brought about. The Lord is full of compassion and mercy.

¹²Above all, my brothers, do not swear—not by heaven or by earth or by anything else. Let your "Yes" be yes, and your "No," no, or you will be condemned.

Questions

OPEN: 1. When have you and your community experienced the effects of a drought? Of too much rain? **2.** What do you think of as "the good ole days" in your life? Were they really that good?

DIG: 1. Instead of retaliating or seeking vengeance, what are the poor to do? Why? **2.** What lessons are provided by the farmer? By the returning Judge? By the prophets? By Job? By the call to integrity (v.12)?

REFLECT: 1. When you experience hardship, what enables you to be patient and wait for God? What has really tested that? **2.** Have you ever gone through a period when you doubted God's presence in the midst of hardship and suffering? Explain.

Notes

5:7-12 James' argument is finished. He has said what he wants to say about testing (and temptation), about wisdom (and speech), and about riches (and generosity). Now all that remains is for him to conclude his book by summarizing his points. However, he does not do this in a neat, systematic way. Rather, he simply alludes to each theme in the midst of offering final encouragement to the church in Jerusalem.

5:7-11 It has been very difficult for the church in Jerusalem. The times are hard. There is famine. There is poverty. Being Christians, they have received little of the general relief donated by wealthy Jewish aristocrats living outside Palestine. Then there is the persecution which has pushed them down even further. So they are weary. When will the trials end? When will Christ return? Their hard situation had worn them down so that they are slipping from Christ's way into the ways of the world. "Hold on," James says, "stand firm, be like Job. Jesus will return."

5:7-8 James begins this concluding section by summarizing his ideas about testing. **patient**. This word (and its derivatives) are the most frequently used words in the passage. The basic idea is that of *patient waiting*. It is related to the endurance that James commended in 1:3 ("perseverance"), though patience connotes a more passive holding on than the active endurance of chapter 1. **until**. Such patient waiting on the part of the poor is possible because they know that an event is coming that will radically change their situation, namely the Lord's return. **See how the farmer waits**. In due course, the rains will come. In the meantime, the farmer can do nothing to hasten or delay their arrival. He must simply wait for the gift of rain. **for the land to yield**. Likewise, he must wait for the land to give forth a crop. Once he has sowed his seed (apart from pulling our weeds and and keeping birds and animals away), there is nothing the farmer can do. Growth, too, is a gift. **valuable**. This was literally his most precious possession. Without a crop he would have nothing to sell or barter. Even worse, he and his family would starve. **stand firm**. While waiting, the tempta-

tion will be to slip into inappropriate survival modes—specifically in this case, that of adopting the methods of the world (e.g., revenge). The longer they wait, the stronger the temptation to doubt the Second Coming, and even to doubt the Christian faith itself. They must resist these temptations. **near**. The common feeling in the New Testament days was that the Lord's return was imminent—any day now (see Ro 13:11-12).

5:9 James now touches on the theme of speech. **grumble**. This word is literally "groan." While groaning in the face of suffering is appropriate (see Mk 7:34 and Ro 8:23), groaning at one another is not!

5:10-11 From the theme of speech, James moves back to the theme of trials and tests. **take the prophets**. James does not have to mention by name all the men and women who spoke truth in God's name and suffered for it. In this oral culture, versed in Scripture, all he has to do is to make a reference and the people will think of the stories by themselves.

5:11 persevered. At this point, James shifts from the more passive word "patience" to the idea of active endurance of suffering, a concept which describes Job's experience. **finally brought about**. But in the end, God blessed Job with far more than he had at the beginning of his trials (Job 42:10-17). The implications of this are clear: if they will hold on ("stand firm"), their reward too will be great. **The Lord is full of compassion and mercy**. An allusion to Psalm 103:8 or 111:4. God does not enjoy seeing people suffer. He will intervene in the fullness of time.

5:12 James shifts back to the tongue. This is the first of a series of commandments by which he will end his letter, each of which have to do with how to live while waiting for Jesus to return. **swear**. The issue is not that of using foul language but of taking an oath to guarantee a promise. The extraordinary amount of oath-taking in those days was an indication of how wide-spread lying and cheating was. (Honest people need no oaths.)

59

UNIT 12   The Prayer of Faith

James 5:13-20

The Prayer of Faith

¹³Is any one of you in trouble? He should pray. Is anyone happy? Let him sing songs of praise. ¹⁴Is any one of you sick? He should call the elders of the church to pray over him and anoint him with oil in the name of the Lord. ¹⁵And the prayer offered in faith will make the sick person well; the Lord will raise him up. If he has sinned, he will be forgiven. ¹⁶Therefore confess your sins to each other and pray for each other so that you may be healed. The prayer of a righteous man is powerful and effective.

¹⁷Elijah was a man just like us. He prayed earnestly that it would not rain, and it did not rain on the land for three and a half years. ¹⁸Again he prayed, and the heavens gave rain, and the earth produced its crops.

¹⁹My brothers, if one of you should wander from the truth and someone should bring him back, ²⁰remember this: Whoever turns a sinner from the error of his way will save him from death and cover over a multitude of sins.

Questions

OPEN: As a child, did you pray before you went to bed at night? If so, did you pray a set prayer every night, or did you talk conversationally? Who taught you to pray?

DIG:1. What lessons about prayer is James highlighting in verses 13-18? How is the example of Elijah meant as an encouragement to those addressed in verses 13-16 (see notes)? **4.** From this book, what are some ways "wandering from the truth" (v.19) has been demonstrated in this community? What has James done to try to bring them back?

REFLECT:1. When have you come the closest to wandering from the faith? What (or who) helped bring you back? How does that demonstrate the healing ministry of the Body of Christ? How would you help someone else come back to the faith? **3.** What is the connection between the spiritual, emotional, physical, vocational, and relational areas of our lives? Can a person be sick or sinful in one area and be completely whole in the others? Conversely, can one regain health in one area and not have that spill over into other areas? Why or why not? **4.** The book of James can polarize those who grapple with it. Which way do you find yourself leaning: Guilty or inspired? Resistant or repentant? Passing the buck to the rich, or passing out bucks to the poor? **5.** How can you be a "doer" of the truth you have heard in James?

Notes

5:13-20 In literary epistles such as this one (according to Peter Davids), it is customary to end with three items: an oath, a health wish, and the purpose for writing. James has each of these. In verse 12, oaths are mentioned (though not in the traditional way). James does not offer an oath to guarantee the truth of this letter. He rejects all oaths! In 5:13-18 there is a health wish, as James instructs them in how to obtain health through prayer. And then finally, he sums up the purpose of his letter in 5:19-20. His aim has been to warn sinners of their erroneous ways.

5:13-18 The theme of this section is prayer. Prayer is the form of speech that James commends most highly in his letter. However, James also identifies two other forms of speech which ought to characterize Christians: singing (v.13) and confession of sins (v.16). Such proper speech contrasts with the two forms of improper speech identified in the previous section: grumbling (v.8) and oath-taking (v.12). In this way, James summarizes his teaching on speech while at the same time extending it to new areas.

5:14-15 There is a long tradition of faith healing in the Christian church. *sick*. It is one thing to be persecuted, to be hungry, or to fight with other church members. These problems stem from the evil that is in the world. But illness is another matter. It is not something anybody else does to you. Especially in the first century, illness made one feel so vulnerable. What could you do? Where could you go for help? James has an answer. *call the elders*. Illness was to be dealt with in the context of the Christian community. The elders— the council that ran the church—were to be called to minister to the ill person. They had two things to do: to pray over the person and to anoint him or her with oil. *anoint him with oil*. When a Jew was ill, he or she first went to a rabbi to be anointed with oil. Oil was used not only for ritual purposes but for cleaning wounds, for paralysis, and for toothaches. In this case, the olive oil is not being used as a medicine but as a part of the healing prayer (see Mk 6:13 and Lk 10:34).

5:15 *prayer offered in faith*. James has discussed this kind of prayer already (see 1:5-8 and 4:1-3.) His point is that "without the life of commitment to God that the prayer expresses, it will be ineffectual. The faith lies in the elders, not in the sick person (about whose faith nothing is said). The elders' faith is critical: If something 'goes wrong' it is they, not the sick person, who bear the onus" (Davids, GNC). *the Lord will raise him up*. James is quite clear about the source of the healing. It is not the oil, it is not the laying on of hands by the elders, nor is it even prayer in some sort of magical sense. It is God who heals. *sinned*. Traditional Judaism maintained that there was a connection between sin and illness: "No sick person is cured of his disease until all his sins are forgiven him" (Babylonian Talmud). In this sense, healing would be a confirmation that God had also forgiven the sins that were confessed (see Mk 2:1-12). Though James does not teach an inevitable connection between sin and illness, he suggests that at times this may be the case, much as modern medicine has recognized that illness is often a product of wrong living (psychosomatic illness).

5:16 *confess your sins*. Confessing your sins to one another removes barriers between people and promotes honesty in the Christian community. *to each other*. This is not an action to be taken only when one is ill (and then only with the elders). Public confession of sins is for everyone. *powerful and effective*. It is not that prayer is an independent force (like magic incantations). Prayer is directed to *God*, who is all-powerful and who works in this world.

5:19-20 James concludes his letter by summarizing its purpose. *wander*. Christian truth captivates not only the mind, but one's whole life, including how one lives. This is the point of James' letter. Hence James can speak about wandering from Christian truth, presumably into other styles of living. It is not primarily doctrinal deviation that has concerned James. It is how one lives.

ACKNOWLEDGEMENTS

In writing these notes, use has been made of the standard exegetical tools—Bible dictionaries, lexicons, word studies, background studies and a variety of commentaries. In this regard, particular note must be made of two books by Peter H. Davids. These were published after I had completed the first draft of the manuscript. In the revision process they proved to be invaluable, clearing up a host of questions, giving me a new feel for the overall structure of the book, and in general serving as models of good scholarship linked to passionate concern for the truth of what is in the Book of James. One of Dr. Davids' books is written for a general audience and it would be an excellent resource to use along with this material. It is entitled simply *James* and is part of the *Good News Commentary* series published in 1983 by Harper and Row (hereafter abbreviated as GNC). The second volume is a more technical study and requires some familiarity with Greek. It will be of special value to the pastor who is teaching this course. Its title is *Commentary on James* and it is part of the *New International Greek Testament Commentary* series, published in 1982 by the William B. Eerdmans Publishing Company (hereafter abbreviated as NIGTC).

Two other commentaries were of special value: *The Epistle of James* by Sophie Laws (Harper's New Testament Commentaries), New York: Harper and Row, 1980 and *The Letters of James and Peter* by William Barclay (The Daily Study Bible), Philadelphia: The Westminster Press, 1960. Both the Laws and Barclay volumes contained a wealth of historical detail and background data.

Reference was also made to *The Epistle of James* (The New International Commentary on the New Testament), by James Adamson, Grand Rapids: William B. Eerdmans Publishing Co., 1976; *James* by Marilyn Kunz and Catherine Schell (Neighborhood Bible Studies), Wheaton: Tyndale House Publishers; *The Tests of Faith* by J.A. Motyer, London: Inter-Varsity Press, 1970; *The Epistles of James, Peter, and Jude* by Bo Reicke (The Anchor Bible), Garden City, NY: Doubleday & Co., 1964; *A Critical and Exegetical Commentary on the Epistle of St. James* by James Hardy Ropes (The International Critical Commentary), Edinburgh: T. & T. Clark, 1978; *The General Epistle of James* by R.V.G. Tasker (Tyndale New Testament Commentaries), London: The Tyndale Press, 1956; and *The Letters of John and James* by R. R. Williams (The Cambridge Bible Commentary), Cambridge at the University Press, 1965.